Prelude
to
Tomorrow

Cody & Chase –

Happy Travels!

Prelude
to
Tomorrow

A Collection of Travel Stories

Paul Hudson

iUniverse, Inc.
New York Lincoln Shanghai

Prelude to Tomorrow
A Collection of Travel Stories

iUniverse books may be ordered through booksellers or by contacting:

iUniverse
2021 Pine Lake Road, Suite 100
Lincoln, NE 68512
www.iuniverse.com
1-800-Authors (1-800-288-4677)

Because of the dynamic nature of the Internet, any Web addresses or links contained in this book may have changed since publication and may no longer be valid.

The views expressed in this work are solely those of the author and do not necessarily reflect the views of the publisher, and the publisher hereby disclaims any responsibility for them.

ISBN: 978-0-595-46249-0 (pbk)
ISBN: 978-0-595-70044-8 (cloth)
ISBN: 978-0-595-90549-2 (ebk)

Printed in the United States of America

To Cullum

Contents

Part III   Europe

Part IV   Lake Tahoe

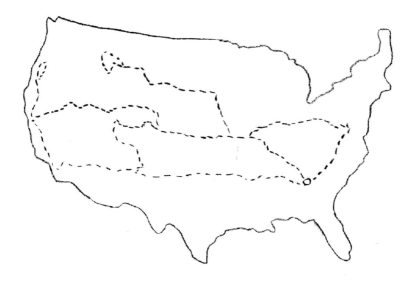

Preface

The windows in the truck were rusted open. My arms were hanging out the window; I felt hypnotized by the muddled hum of rubber wearing on the pavement. The fences were briskly rolling by beside the road. Had it ever rained in this town? This must be the place. Was I here? Was this the street of my imagination?

My local ride treated the hitch into town as if he were picking up his buddy. The second I jumped in, he started chatting. We apparently had an interrupted conversation just minutes before that needed finishing. Only I'd never met the man before in my life. As I stared out the window, watching the distant town gradually approaching, my new friend kept talking up a storm, with great concentration. At each break in the monologue, I asked brief questions to remain engaged in conversation. The one-word questions were usually short and to the point, which was to allow him to catch his breath before moving on with his story. Then he was off again to the races. After talking at length about a rustic farm down the valley that he'd had his eye on for years, he paused abruptly to notice a new song playing on the radio, a bluegrass tune. I naively asked if any good music ever came to town. This started him right back up again with a jolt.

"Oh, you should have seen it, man—the town was packed a week in advance. We've always had blue skies and beautiful women, but as far as music, we had David Grisman, Peter Rowan, Bela Fleck and the Flecktones, Tony Rice, Jerry Douglas ..." He then stopped to take a breath of air. "It's pretty sweet, man—you should check it out sometime."

Snapping out of a newly inflicted daydream, I tore my eyes from the face of the mountain. With a look of sudden enlightenment, I slowly peered across the truck in his direction. My reply was one of simple conviction: "Yeah, I think I will." This was followed by a nod of assurance and then a more affirmative, "Yeah, I will." I meant it, too. *You damn well better believe it.* With that, I closed my eyes, head tilting back, as I looked out across my life into the future.

The festival, of course, was the famous Telluride Bluegrass Festival. How had I not known? How was it that people had gathered in the Telluride valley every summer since 1974 to listen to good ole country rootin' bluegrass, without the gospel spreading my way? Perhaps I was slowly starting to realize that there were pursuits in the world that were not on the agenda of my parents. I was now of the persuasion that any week when the Bluegrass Festival was not happening was an inopportune time to visit Telluride. Although I had to face the fact that I had missed the festival that summer, it sparked an idea.

My uncle Ben, a story-telling uncle, once told me long tales of the trips he took in his youthful days of exploration. One was a hippie-type tale about traveling west in a Volkswagen van. Another was more of a self-discovery story about a personal sojourn throughout Europe. This concept of extensive travel caught my interest. I decided to plan a trip of my own. My trip would naturally include a stop at the Telluride Bluegrass Festival.

A year later, my good friends Chas Smithgall, Donald Houser, Justin Rainer, and I were to embark on a three-week Western road trip that opened our eyes to the broader world. We were ecstatic to explore the depths of the United States, a nation that we seemed to love, yet didn't really know. The summer provided us with our first real experience with freedom—absent of adult guidance.

I quickly became fond of this concept of freedom and travel. In fact, I kept the train rolling. Each summer thereafter, as soon as I was able, I took off to explore the world.

The following is an account of my travels throughout the American West, Africa, and Europe. Yet this is not just a story of travel.

This is a story of friendship and of youth. It is a story that we all know, for we have all been though it. This story just happens to be mine, that's all. The events are as true as my memory will allow. The conversations surely did not occur word for word as presented, yet this is how I remember them—they are true to me. If not in action, the words are true in spirit, at a minimum.

If you are merely reading this preface to gauge your potential interest in these so-called tales of adventure, and if, in fact, you never turn another page and you return this book to the shelf, and if you are to only learn one thing, then I leave you with this:

Drive across the country with your friends. There is no possible way that you will regret it. You learn a great deal about freedom, a great deal about your friends, and a great deal about yourself. I didn't think it would be possible for the four of us to become better friends. Needless to say, we did. Donald, Justin, Chas, and I took part in remarkable dreams that we'll share for the rest of our lives—fishing the streams of the West, camping under the stars, biking in the desert sun, roaming endless country roads—the list goes on. It isn't so much that you learn new information about your friends when you take a trip. We knew pretty much everything there was to know. But we shared an experience that no one else will understand or appreciate as much as we can. That is what's important. And I just thought you might like to hear about it.

I know. This is going to be good.

PART I

Go West, My Son, Go West

1

Departing Georgia

The line was out the door when we got to Jalisco's. Then again, when was it not?

"Oh, hey Paul—how many?" said Rosanne as I shuffled through.

"We've got four tonight." Four always seemed to be the number.

"Mom, Dad, and Taylor?"

"No, Justin, Chas, and Donald."

Justin then squeezed by and tapped me on the shoulder.

"How's it look?" he asked, as he saw Rosanne in front of me.

"Hey, Justin," she said, "Shouldn't be but just a few minutes."

"Cool, we'll be outside; you know where to find us."

It was only fitting that we ate at Jalisco's the night before the big trip. The neighborhood Mexican restaurant was our home away from home. I'd been eating at Jalisco's once a week since I could walk. My parents carried me in before that. The routine was the same for all of us. Eating at Jalisco's in Atlanta was equivalent in ritual to going to church. It was just a part of life, I guess. For one thing, they have the best damn salsa and cheese dip in America. You can thank the Lord for that.

"Do ya'll really want to wait in line?" asked Chas. "I heard some people were going to Fellini's." Chas had a problem with committing to an idea, especially when something else seemed to be brewing.

This comment frustrated Donald. "Chas, just chill for a minute; you know it goes quick." Donald could be as restless as Chas, but once he made up his mind, it was set in stone.

"I'm also kind of in the mood for a beer," Chas thought out loud. "I don't want to order one with all these parents around."

Justin jumped in, "Chas, they know damn well we aren't twenty-one. Let's just wait it out, we're almost up."

Rosanne sat us in a booth in the second room, near the window.

"What time do we have to get up tomorrow?" This was a common concern of Justin's.

"7:00 AM," I said, "We need to get on the road early."

"Liquor store doesn't open till 9:00 AM," Chas said casually.

"Good point," I replied. "We can sleep till 8:00 AM, I guess."

"I'm nervous about driving with liquor," said Donald. "It's a long way out there."

"Exactly." said Justin. "A long way, and we don't know where to buy it once we get there. In Atlanta, I can tell you five places."

"Donald, I think we'll be all right," I said. "I don't like it either, but they make a good point."

"We better hide it well then," Donald concluded.

"We will; I've got a good spot for it," I said. "We won't break it out until the festival."

Donald seemed to come around. "This trip is going to be sweet," he said. "I haven't been out West in forever. We're always in Hilton Head."

"I can't believe ya'll go to that same beach every summer," said Chas. "Don't you get bored?"

"Houser knows Hilton Head sucks," said Justin. "Seaside is where it's at."

"Seaside's just as bad. Don't ya'll ever want to get around more?" Chas was being persistent.

Donald stated the obvious. "Chas, your family is the only one I know that has an unlimited Delta pass. It's not like the rest of us can hop on a plane at our whim." Chas's mom was a flight attendant who had retired with some killer benefits.

"Maybe every family should be *required* to have a flight attendant," I said. "Not a bad gig, if you ask me."

Justin jumped in. "The last trip my family took away from the beach was a five-day horse trek in Canada. It started hailing forty-five minutes into the trip. Then it turned to snow. This was the middle of summer. My parents prefer Seaside."

"Horses? My mom wouldn't dream of getting on a horse," said Donald. "Away from the beach, our family did take that one big trip to Europe, I guess, but I'm not even sure if I was invited."

"Houser, don't worry," said Chas, "We've got plenty of time to take some cool trips. I'm just pumped about this one. Damn, I can't wait to get out there."

"Ya'll are going to love Telluride," I said. "May be one of the coolest places I've ever been."

"You always say that, Hudson," said Donald with a laugh.

I smiled. What could I say? I guess I have been to some cool spots.

The mental picture of my parents waving good-bye as we drove away that early June morning makes me laugh a little. I wonder what they were thinking as we departed. Were their thoughts about the upcoming trip the same as ours? I'm sure there were differences in mindset.

Our parents have watched the four of us grow up together our entire lives. Essentially, Donald, Justin, and I have been best friends since birth. Because of our parents' friendship before we were born, it was never in question that we would also be friends. In fact, it was out of our hands completely. Even before we could speak, we seemed to strangely understand that we were brothers—not by birth, yet brothers nonetheless. We met Chas shortly thereafter in preschool. Our families lived within a mile of each other, a convenience that only aided our friendship.

Growing up, we were vastly different individuals. Donald was the mischievous one in the early years. Always tinkering with the boundaries of the acceptable, he taught us the ways of the world (as taught to him by his older brother). The older-brother factor made Donald an expert on everything that we didn't know. You see, Justin, Chas, and I were firstborn children. We were on our own to determine appropriate conduct and behavior. But Donald had a teacher. His brother was eager to teach Donald the next steps in life, which, of course, Donald was keen to share as well.

Justin was a quick learner. Donald would show us the concepts, and Justin would run with them. Chas and I tended to just sit back and absorb it all. Usually, I was not the one to start up any trouble. But I can't say I wasn't often there when the trouble took place. I guess I've always been intrigued by it, but never wanted to be the instigator.

As the years went by, Donald outgrew his devious nature and settled comfortably into conformity. He recently graduated as the editor and chief of the law review at Washington and Lee. Justin, on the other hand, has always been the stubborn one of the four. He isn't one for following the normal path, but that's where his brilliance lies, and we love him for it. As Donald has been familiarizing himself with the law, Justin has been off on the slopes of Jackson Hole—trying to escape reality for as long as possible.

In conversation, I'm often the quiet one of the group. People tend to write me off as practical and conservative, straight and narrow. That is, until they get to know me. Growing up, I was that annoying kid who did exactly as he was told, which pissed off my friends to no end. To this day, I'm not sure what made me behave that way, always staying in the center of the herd. But because of that, deep down I'm a dreamer—steady and constant in my actions, but wild in thought.

In some ways, Chas may be the most interesting of the four, simply because you never know what you're going to get out of Chas. You see, he doesn't seem to know either. Chas is an adaptor of ideas. He watches us all very carefully, often asking us questions about our behavior, not because he is *critical,* necessarily, but because he's curious as to why we make the decisions that we do. Once he sees our decisions pan out, Chas takes a step back to contemplate the best path, and then runs to catch up in that direction. Chas and I have been on a very similar path in life, which I take as a tremendous compliment, as it means Chas must think I have pretty good taste. But I'm getting ahead of myself now, aren't I? There's a long tale to tell.

As I mentioned, the morning after Jalisco's, the four of us had a little trip to go on. We were jazzed. There's nothing better than an excursion.

Colorado-bound, we took a right out of my driveway onto West Wesley Road and headed toward the interstate. Once out on the open road, we quickly found the far left lane of the highway and called it home.

"What do ya'll want to hear?" asked Chas.

"Allman Brothers," said Donald.

"Good call," I said. I was glad we were all on the same page.

We then settled down into comfort and began the gradual practice of easing the mind. The intended goal, for that particular day, was to sleep in St. Louis, Missouri.

The first few hours were possibly the best. The mood was of the better type—laughter was a good sign of our collective spirit. I was especially excited, as an entire year had passed since my idea for the cross-country excursion. And there's something about traveling west that just makes you feel adventurous. As you can imagine, the windows were down, and the sky was blue. The feeling overwhelmed me that we were on the road problem free—until Tennessee, that is.

When you picture driving out West, or taking any trip, for that matter, you don't ever think about the things that can go wrong. That's because you can never predict what they will be. We never would have guessed this one. We were three hours outside of Atlanta, on a thirty-hour trip to our first long stop, when suddenly one of my dashboard lights lit up. Not one of the gas lights, or even the oil lights, but one of those lights that you've never even seen before: "Check Engine." Great. The one thing we needed was a working car, and working cars need engines. And by the way, *check engine*? What the hell does that even mean, anyway? How do you check an engine?

We even got out and checked the damn thing, and it looked fine. So we checked—now what?

"Dad."

"Hey … how's the drive? How far have ya'll gone?"

"We're a little outside Chattanooga."

"How's the traffic?"

"Not bad. Dad, we've got a problem."

"Ya'll okay?"

"Yeah, but my Check Engine light just came on."

"Check Engine? Have ya'll looked at it?"

"Yeah, we *looked* at it. Looking doesn't seem to help."

But the car felt fine to drive. We continued on our way to St. Louis, yet not at the desirable speed. We didn't want to push the car too hard, given the circumstances. It turned out not to be a major problem, but it was an interesting start to the trip, nonetheless.

Chattanooga appeared to be the tobacco capital of the world. Every other store was a tobacco outlet.

"I wonder if they have Drum tobacco," I mused.

"Since when have you smoked, Hudson?" Justin asked. He knew damn well I didn't smoke. Justin probably knew my behavioral pattern as well as anyone.

"I don't, but maybe I would if we had Drum tobacco."

"Why?" asked Chas.

"I don't know; might be cool to smoke out of a pipe."

Justin said, "Ya'll remember when Donald used to make us smoke pine straw?"

"You mean *puffers*?" Donald said, with an enthusiastic grin.

"Yes! Puffers." This brought Chas to life.

Puffers were an invention that Donald and his brother thought up when we were about twelve years old. You would take a handful of pine straw, wrap it tightly in a piece of paper, light it up, and puff on it until a cloud of smoke came out. They served no other purpose than for us to look cool and act older than our age. When we were kids, it was not rare on a summer afternoon to find the four of us wandering through the woods behind Donald's house, puffers in one hand, and some sort of bush-whacking stick in the other, blazing trails and building forts near the creek. If you asked us, we would've told you we were deep in the jungle, even though we were only about a hundred yards from the street.

After a deep exploration of our neighborhoods, and as we got older, we slowly started to realize that there was more to discover in the world than the woods behind our houses—hence the motivation for our current trip.

Later that afternoon, we were each silent and apparently deep in thought, mesmerized by the rolling Kentucky hills.

"Ya'll remember the last time we all went out West?" asked Donald.

"Skiing?" said Justin.

"No," said Chas. "It was OWA. What was that, ninth grade?"

"Yeah," I responded. "I also went back a year later with Preston."

Outpost Wilderness Adventures was a camp in Colorado, about two hours west of Colorado Springs. The four of us, plus a few other close friends, went there for two weeks one summer to mountain bike, backpack, and rock climb. When we were fifteen, the forests of Colorado were the perfect playground.

"Houser, you still a rock climber?" Chas asked jokingly. Donald was a tackle in football, not a natural fit for the sport.

"No," he responded, "but I think Salsa would still kick Rainer's ass in mountain biking." Salsa was our nickname for Justin's archrival at the camp. Salsa was from Aspen, which naturally gave him a leg up on the trail.

"Bullshit," said Justin. "I'll show you I still got it when we get to Moab."

We were not the most athletic bunch when it came to normal sports, but we were much more active than most in the outdoors. You wouldn't ever find us on the basketball court, but if you searched hard enough you could probably find us in the woods somewhere (likely on our mountain bikes). During high school at The Westminster

Schools, Donald and I were tennis players during the spring. Donald was difficult to beat, not because of the strength of his shots, or his accuracy, but because he was so damn consistent. It was quite boring to play Donald in tennis, and often frustrating (especially when you were losing).

Chas picked up lacrosse as his sports venture. I can't say he was a natural, but he seemed to like running around with a stick and hitting people who weren't looking, so it was a good fit.

As with all groups of friends, we were competitive, although the sports arena was not usually the venue for the competition.

On occasion, we attempted to battle it out in school. Not that I could compete in the left-brain subjects. But I made up ground in English and History. Donald loved the competition in school. In fact, he still does. He is somewhat a professional student.

My competition with Justin never flared up on a specific basis, but it was always beneath the surface—an ongoing gradual fight around who could be better at everything. You see, our fathers were partners at a local law firm called Parker, Hudson, Rainer & Dobbs. From an early age, Justin and I would compare our fathers to one another, and from there it only made sense that we take it a step further and judge ourselves.

Unfortunately for me, Justin was a natural in the area in which our competition was most prevalent—on the ski slopes. Justin was an inch or two taller than I was, and much skinnier, so he was better fit for the activities that required frequent agility. He was also apparently much more attractive than I was, which is the killer of all killers. I can't tell you the number of times that I would be talking to a girl, when she would interrupt me to ask where Justin was, who he was dating, etc. That's the oldest way in the book to get the competitive juices going!

But the four of us were the best of friends. I was ecstatic the morning we departed for Colorado, for the thought that we were about to spend three weeks traveling the West together was almost too much for me to bear.

Of course, we were glad to see the St. Louis arches that first evening. I was the only person in the car who didn't require Ritalin on a daily basis, which gives you an idea of how restless the others were after nine hours in the car.

Donald shared a theory about where we should sleep in St. Louis. The theory went something like this: the north side of all cities is always the nice side. Think about it. Most major cities are built along or near a large river. Once a city is built, all of its activity ends up polluting the river. Therefore, in the early days when people first started settling a city, the area to the south was considered worse than the north, since its water source has been polluted from the construction. You will typically find that the early inhabitants of cities will build the nice houses on the north side for that reason. And once the nice area is established, it stays that way. So, the nice side of a city is always going to be the north side. This is especially true for cities right *on* the water, like St. Louis.

Now, I haven't checked the theory to see if it has any merit, or holes in its deductive reasoning, but to me it seems to make sense. And that was all of the sense that we needed that night, since we really had no idea what St. Louis was like. So, we drove through the south side (which no one wanted to admit looked pretty nice) and made our way into the northern section, only to discover the slums. Great theory, Donald!

If you've never taken a long road trip—and I don't mean a four- to five-hour drive, but an all-day expedition where you can't remember if you've ever *not* been in the car before—then trust me when I tell you that you greatly value any time outside of the car's walls. The gas and piss stops are nice. But they're nothing compared to the moments when you can sit down for a while and eat a meal. That night we were starving. We also were in the mood for something good. This is relatively easy to find in your own city. Yet finding good food in an unfamiliar one is a very tough thing to do.

After a respectable-looking father in a newly washed Mercedes sent us to a place which just didn't look right, we eventually made our way into a college area that seemed to have a few prospects. We asked a guy crossing the street, who appeared to know the place, for a good dinner spot. He seemed all right. I was willing to go with his opinion when he offered it.

"Excuse me. We're not from around here. We're looking for a good place to eat."

"Oh yeah … umm …" He looked around for a good ten seconds until his eye caught a new sign. "Oh," he said, "there's a great fresh Mexican place right over there. The food's really good." The sign above the door said Fresh Mexican.

"Oh, okay," I said, "yeah, that looks good, thanks."

We were hungry enough to accept his advice and walked into the suspiciously uncrowded restaurant. It was time for a little relaxation and to plan out the next day's drive.

The food was terrible. I could tell upon the first bite. You see, Chas gets these looks on his face which tell us that he's extremely annoyed, and after seeing one of these looks form, I knew immediately what he was going to say. "Is ya'll's food any good?" He said that with a look of disgust.

This was Justin's cue. "This place sucks. How does that guy like this place?"

After eating our unsatisfying meals, we headed back inside to pay.

"What'd you think guys? How was the food?"

"It was good. Thanks." I wasn't in the mood to tell him the truth.

"Oh, I'm glad. You guys are our first customers. We just opened up for our grand opening tonight." We all looked at each other, with smirks that wanted to say, "Oh really, good luck making it a week." And where's that guy with the great recommendation?

The next day we got on the road early, turned west on I-70, and continued in one direction—straight. A friend of ours, Brooks, had driven out to Denver on a fly-fishing trip with his father the previous summer. We asked him about the drive. He said it was fine, except that Kansas was extremely boring. So my heart sank a little once when we reached the sign welcoming us to the dull state of Kansas. Brooks had no idea what he was talking about!

It was great driving through Kansas. Miles and miles of never-ending farmland taunted our eyes to try to look as far into the distance as possible. There were no obstacles in sight marking the end to the view. It didn't seem feasible that there was so much open space without even a building. The contrast of the blue sky with the wheat fields was a cool sight.

I was excited that we got to admire that scenery all the way to Colorado. Driving through the western part of the country sparked an unusual feeling. It was almost as if the world was one big panoramic picture that you could roll down like a window and put your arm into. Actually, never mind that. The world *is* one big panoramic picture that you put your arm into. At least, that's a better thing on the road than it is in most crowded cities.

The morning was clear and blue. I gazed out the window in a trance, as Justin drove beside me.

"Damn, check out those windmills," said Justin, to break the silence.

"We're in the middle of nowhere," I responded. "Feels nice to get away."

"Are Chas and Houser asleep?" I looked back, and they had both nodded off, heads resting against the windows.

"Yeah, taking a nap, looks like."

"I can't believe ya'll are going to be gone next year," said Justin.

"I know; weird, isn't it?" I replied.

"Doesn't seem right. Who am I going to hang out with?" Justin was a month older than me, but I was a grade ahead in school. Chas, Donald, and I had graduated only weeks before. Justin had one more year to go.

"Just come visit us a lot," I suggested. I felt a little bad for Justin, but he had a good crew of friends who would keep him busy. "You should spend some time with Houser in Athens this fall," I said. "Only an hour away. Girls are gorgeous too."

"Yeah," Justin replied, "I'll probably head over to Tuscaloosa as well."

"You dead set on going to Bama?" I knew the answer but always liked to check.

"My parents would kill me if I looked anywhere else."

Chas had apparently woken up during the conversation.

"Maybe I should go to Bama with you," Chas mumbled.

"Thought you were asleep," said Justin. "Not excited about Vandy?"

"Not really," Chas said. "Never pictured myself there, I guess." After a brief pause, Chas spoke up again. "Hudson, were you ready to finish high school?"

"What do you mean?" I asked.

"I don't know. I mean, did you feel ready? I was having a good time. Wasn't really ready to move on yet."

"I don't know. I guess so. I'm never really ready to move on, but I always seem to like the next phase when it comes. I'm pretty pumped for Charlottesville."

"I would be too," said Chas. "I guess that's the problem. I'm not excited about where I'm going."

"Vanderbilt will be cool," I said. "Bunch of hotties there as well, I hear."

"That's going to have to get me through it," Chas responded. "Ya'll up for lunch yet?"

Stopping for lunch in a small town, we hoped to find a classic country-type spot instead of settling for fast food. Although the highway sign only informed us of a closed restaurant, we soon realized that the exit we had taken was well worth exploring.

A dirt road led us deeper into the countryside, as it mirrored the path of train tracks. Upon the sight of silos, country fences, run-down signs, and wheat (a ton of it), the notion first sank in that we were actually in the midst of the Great Plains.

Now don't be *too* jealous. I know that the Kansas wheat fields aren't exactly the most sought-after destination in our country. I'll have to check, but they may actually be the least. However, they were new to us, and were, believe it or not, enthralling. Perhaps we couldn't comprehend how in-the-middle-of-nowhere we actually were. The thought crossed my mind, and it seemed pretty legitimate at the time, that if we kept walking to the end of the field we were standing in, we'd probably end up in another state, hundreds of miles away. Kansas leaves you with that type of feeling. I realized that the others were thinking similar thoughts when Justin said, "We should recreate that picture."

There are always a few pictures of your parents that you love to look at. You know the ones. They hint that your parents may have in fact been cooler when they were growing up than you thought they were. Chas' hallway had its fair share of those pictures. There was one in particular that we made an effort to look at every time we went in his house. The picture was a black and white of Chas' dad and his dad's brother, with full beards, lying down on train tracks, in the middle of the Canadian wilderness. We literally thought it was the coolest thing we'd ever seen. I think what made the picture so appealing was that it portrayed an immense sense of relaxation. But underlying that carefree spirit was also the portrayal of escape and ruggedness that one gets when one spends time outdoors. We wanted to recreate the picture. We wanted that to be us.

A good spot on the tracks invited us over. We posed, in an attempt to capture the essence of what we were trying to imitate. The pictures turned out well, but didn't quite fulfill their potential. The pictures were in color. Actually, the main problem was that our bright shirts screamed city, and our young faces yearned to grow even chicken scratch for beards.

People sometimes ask, like confused dogs turning their heads in question, what the hell we were doing in those pictures. I usually say something different each time. The situation is a little hard to explain. But I want to keep taking pictures as long as I travel, and a lot of them too, in hope of capturing our own moments that someone may wish to recreate on *their* travels.

There's something about a well-taken picture and the things that it expresses that brings out the jealous nature in all of us. And while jealousy of others' possessions is one of the most unhealthy habits, jealousy of others' experiences can be very healthy if it drives us to experience more in our own lives. If we can relate to a picture, it reminds us about who are and where we've been. But even if we can't relate, we enjoy getting one step closer to understanding the captured moment.

Later that day, as the sky began to darken for both the night and a coming storm, we continued our search for a local haven at which to dine. We couldn't find exactly what we wanted, but ended up eating at a place that was both a restaurant and a gas station. We figured that had to fulfill some kind of road trip requirement, and at least got us points for something. Eventually, we looked up from our mediocre hamburgers to realize that all the occupants of the restaurant seemed to be eating rather quickly. Given the quality of the food, there had to be another explanation. We slowly began to understand why.

The people staring at the sky caught our attention. It was getting *extremely* dark. It was not yet time for the sun to have set. Justin and I went outside to check out the situation for ourselves. There was no wind whatsoever. Sign one: it actually felt so still that it left you standing a little uncomfortably. Sign two: that discomfort grew when you looked up and noticed that half of the sky was pretty light, and then turned to see what looked like death's blanket hovering in the sky. Unfortunately, the blanket appeared as if it were trying to tuck us into bed. If you went to sleep under that thing, you wouldn't wake up.

There was a lady standing a few feet away, looking upward, with her head tilted back, eyes wide open, and jaw dropped in amazement. We walked over to gather her thoughts.

She began, "Have you boys ever been in a tornado?"

"No, have you?"

"Yeah. I was in one a few years ago down in Oklahoma."

"Really? What'd it look like?"

"Like that," she said, pointing at the sky.

Great. We were about to drive right into a freaking tornado if we weren't in it already. The lady told us that all of the truckers had stopped driving, since the wind down the road was so fast that it might blow the trucks over. She said we should be okay since we were in a sports utility. *Great, lady ... thanks for the comfort!*

After rapidly paying the check, we decided to get back on the road before the storm got any worse. It did. Justin was driving. He was the most trustworthy behind the wheel. We then began flying down the highway as if we were in a scene from the movie *Twister.* Yet we wanted to be the ones trying to get *away* from the tornado, not the ones chasing it. We knew it was serious when Justin admitted that he was having trouble driving (he never has trouble driving in any conditions). He showed us why when he let go of the wheel. The car almost veered off the road, the wind was so strong. A few minutes later, we'd had enough. We were turning around.

The next exit didn't seem to exist. Apparently it was not possible to turn around. This is equivalent to biking toward a cliff without brakes. After twenty minutes, an exit showed its overdue face and we immediately started heading back. Justin even mentioned driving as far back as Kansas City for the night in order to make sure we'd be out of harm's way (when he was a kid he had a tree fall on his house and he doesn't look forward to storms). Chas wouldn't have it. As I'm sure you're well aware, we swallowed a lot of pride as men when we turned the car around. But we knew that driving as far back as Kansas City was a little ridiculous. And in order to double-check our assumption that we even should turn around, we stopped about half an hour later to see if we could find the weather channel. All of the truckers were inside a small café with their eyes glued to the screen. Our concerns were valid, but the situation wasn't as bad as we'd originally thought. The winds were less than tornado speeds, although only slightly, but they didn't appear to be worsening. With the reassurance from the locals at the café, we turned back around and began the crawl toward Denver again.

An hour or so later, I was taken back by the colorful scenery that the brooding storm left in its wake. As I mentioned, half of the sky was darker than night, and the other half was suspiciously clear. When the sun began to set, the clear sky to the right filled with a powerful, bright orange that made us feel we should head in that direction to find the shortcut to heaven. At the same time, intense streaks of lightning began to fill the dark sky to the left. We were apparently nearing the spot where the underworld met the earth. At one point, I couldn't decide whether to stare at the gorgeous sunset or to focus on the electric storm. I even began taking random pictures of the storm, in hope of catching a streak of lightning with my lens. Although that never happened, of course, I did manage to lean out of the car and take some breathtaking shots of the mythological world outside. After an intense rain set in (but nothing bad enough to make us stop or turn around), we settled back down and began making up some of the lost time that nature's evening sports match had caused us to lose.

I asked, "Justin, you remember that rain in Pisgah?" Justin and I were once on a three-day camping trip in the Pisgah National Forest in North Carolina, when it poured, literally poured, for an entire night, without hesitation. Our guide had forgotten to bring the right tarps, so the ten of us had to cram under one small tarp meant for four people.

"Dude, that was miserable," Justin said. "Kind of fun, though," he added, after giving it some thought.

"How about that rain at OWA?" said Donald.

"You mean when we had to hide under bushes for cover?" asked Chas.

"Yeah," said Donald. "Bushes didn't help much. That was miserable and *not* fun."

"Kind of nice to be in a car, I guess," said Justin. "I just hope I don't drive off the road. Can't see shit."

Around 1:30 AM, the welcome sign appeared that marked our arrival to the mile-high city of Denver, Colorado. This brought a slight sense of shock, along with a greater sense of achievement. My mind simultaneously pictured the distance we had just driven across a U.S. map, and what that section would resemble in a plane thirty thousand feet above ground. The number of times I'd flown into this city, after what used to feel like an excruciatingly long plane flight, was a figure too great to recall. Thus, entering the gateway to the Rockies on wheels made me much more appreciative of our two-day expedition.

I was anxious to continue west into the looming mountains, but there were two places that we felt we needed to see first. I wish I could say there was only one. In fact, we originally only intended to make one stop in Denver. Unfortunately, something drastic occurred in the meantime.

On April 20, 1999, Eric Harris and Dylan Klebold walked into the Columbine High School for the last time. They celebrated Adolf Hitler's birthday by committing a dreadful shooting massacre that left dead twelve students, one teacher, and finally, the shooters themselves. Twenty-three others were wounded.

We weren't sure why we felt the need to see the memorial. We didn't know anyone who died, or even know of anyone who lived in Denver. It may have been that, as students, we felt a connection to the incident, or maybe we felt the need to pay respect as Americans. But I think it went deeper than that. We needed to feel closer to the pain that results from the loss of life through tragedy. Our generation has been separated emotionally from the generations of our parents and older relatives. We have never been personally involved with war or been close to death on a large scale. (Sadly, as I write in the fall of 2002, after 9/11, I cannot say this remains true). Yet up to that point in our lives, we had experienced very few situations that would drive us to question that the world was anything but a rather easygoing place. The Persian Gulf War only penetrated our lives through the images we saw on CNN. The war appeared to be a giant fireworks display. Nothing I saw connected those images to actual deaths. The Oklahoma City bombing widened our consciousness of the existence of evil and gave us a closer look at death on a large scale, yet we were still too young to allow ourselves to feel deeply connected with the event.

Columbine was a different story. We were in high school ourselves at the time. It hurt to watch the news. It hurt to see the pictures of those murdered. It was a war on our nation that America couldn't win. We went to the memorial, first, to see in person that what had happened was real, and then to pray for those who had lost their lives.

As we walked up the hill in Robert F. Clement Park, the large crosses and flowers immediately silenced us. Once the Columbine High School came into view below, we looked at each other in disbelief. For some reason, we knew not to say anything. Yellow police tape surrounded the perimeter. Wooden boards filled the windows that had been shot out. The four of us had assumed that the school would be in better shape. Unknown to us at the time, the repair work and cleanup began only a week before our arrival, since the police and FBI didn't release Columbine back to the school district until the beginning of June.

The news clips raced back through my mind. At some point, I began to feel that we were not right in being there. No one should be there. This wasn't a sight we should be seeing, I thought. People had been murdered in the building we couldn't take our eyes off. This was their place. This was the students' place. This wasn't a place for outsiders to be visiting. Whether or not we had justified reasons to visit the memorial, after a few short minutes we felt the need to leave. I remember Donald looking at me and nodding. He said to the others, "We should go."

After a brief lunch, we managed to put the Columbine tragedy behind us and refocus on the plans for our trip. The second stop that we wanted to make in Denver had a much more positive ambience. We were heading to the Red Rocks amphitheater, a natural, geologically formed, open-air amphitheater located in the Rocky Mountain foothills.

Unfortunately, our visit to Red Rocks was not to actually see a performance, but was rather a visit just to see the place that has seen so many special nights of music. Many of the well-versed music fans with whom I have chatted over the years consider Red Rocks to be the best place they have ever seen live music. Many bands also consider the venue their favorite place to play while on tour. We decided that, even though we weren't going to hear any music, we needed to check the place out.

On arrival, it wasn't hard for us to grasp why so many people consider Red Rocks an extraordinary musical setting. The open-air amphitheater is flanked by two towering rocks, of course red in color, named Creation Rock on the south and Ship Rock on the north. Both Creation Rock and Ship Rock are taller than Niagara Falls. From the top of the amphitheater, you are not only presented with an incredible view of the stage, but also with a view of the entire city of Denver. I can only imagine how the lights of a concert would complement the lights of the city, once the sun falls.

Red Rocks was actually once named as one of the seven wonders of the world. Now, I know what you are thinking. *One of the seven wonders of the world?* I thought that title was reserved for places like the Egyptian pyramids and places in Greece and Mesopotamia that no one can pronounce—so I looked into it.

As it turns out, not only are there different types of "Seven Wonders" lists, such as the Seven Wonders of the Ancient World and the Seven Wonders of the Modern World, but there are also different versions of each list, since no one can seem to agree that our world only has seven wonderful places. Red Rocks, at one point, was one of the Seven Wonders of the Natural World. I couldn't figure out which wonder bumped it off the list, or when, but as of now, the Seven Wonders of the Natural World are Mount Everest, Victoria Falls, the Grand Canyon, the Great Barrier Reef, the northern lights, Paricutin (don't worry; I hadn't heard of it either, but it's a Mexican volcano), and the harbor at Rio de Janeiro. Based on the current list, I'd say Red Rocks deserves to sit on the sidelines, although mentally I'm bumping it up to replace Paricutin, although I'm sure it is a cool volcano.

For those who are interested, the current seven wonders of the modern world are the Suez Canal, the Eiffel Tower, the Alaska Highway, the Golden Gate Bridge, the Empire State Building, the Dneproges Dam in Ukraine, and the Panama Canal. And to give them their due credit, as I stumble upon the list we all learned in school, the Seven Wonders of the Ancient World are the Pyramids of Egypt, the Hanging Gardens of Babylon, the Temple of Artemis at Ephesus, the statue of Zeus at Olympia, the marble tomb of King Mausolus Halicarnassus, the Colossus of Rhodes in the Aegean Sea, and the Pharus of Alexandria. I was a little reassured that there were still some exotic places that I couldn't pronounce on this last list.

The earliest record of Red Rocks' modern discovery was in the Hayden Survey of 1869. The area was first publicly opened under the name The Garden of Angels, in 1906. The owner of the land, John Brisken Walker, turned it into a park in 1914.

John Walker sold this once-natural wonder of the world to the City of Denver in 1928 for forty-five dollars an acre. I guess he needed some cash. I would have kept the place. Aside from being a pleasure for the eyes, the Red Rocks amphitheater has natural acoustics which excite most of the musicians who play there. Mary Garden, one of the first performers at the amphitheater in 1911, remarked that, "Never, in any opera house, the world over, have I found more perfect acoustic properties than those under Creation Rock in the natural auditorium at Mount Morrison. I predict that someday twenty thousand people will assemble there to listen to the world's greatest masterpieces." Good prediction.

There were more people there during the middle of the day than I expected. A band was not scheduled to perform that night, but it didn't seem to matter. Red Rocks was crowded with those merely wishing to walk about and admire its beauty. I was also reminded that the people of Colorado are a much more active breed than most. As I struggled up the stairs, dreadfully out of shape and not yet acclimated to the mountains, I was passed by a man jogging casually up the stairs for exercise. We were there for about half an hour. The entire time this guy was just running up and down the stairs as if he were walking in the park. At the bottom of each set, he would do a few push-ups, just to keep things interesting. And he had a super cool headband on too, which made me even more jealous.

"Hudson, you going to play here one day?" Donald asked, as I was staring at the stage in awe.

"Yeah, right," said Justin. "Not sure if Hudson is up for Red Rocks."

"Whatever, dude. I might rock it here one day." I was still hopeful. "I played a show at The Roxy in Atlanta," I added.

"Yeah, we know," said Justin. I had probably talked that one up too much.

"Hudson's never going to live that down," Chas joked with the others.

Chas continued, "Houser, what are you going to miss about high school? You can't say the library. Georgia is going to have one too." This brought out a good laugh.

Donald defended himself, "Chas, you going to miss that time you totaled your car? What was that, the day after your sixteenth birthday? That was pretty tough."

It was great to have the four of us together. Although I was looking forward to Virginia, I was going to miss these guys—that was for damn sure.

2

The Aspen Life

Before we made our way to Telluride for the Bluegrass Festival, we decided to live the luxurious life, since a certain opportunity was within our reach. This opportunity was the chance to stay at Chas's aunt and uncle's ranch in Aspen for four days, alone.

The crawl up into the Rockies was a familiar one. I was glad to reassure my memory that Highway 70 actually does have curves in it, after taking it across the plains from St. Louis the previous day. There is no actual gate that you pass through when you enter the Rockies, although I assure you that you feel as if there is one. As the hills grow and plains fade, your senses slap you awake, revealing a vastly different world. And then, in a turn, it becomes impossible to imagine that you are anywhere near a flat prairie. Your vision seems to gain a new dimension, one that includes height, and a lot of it.

We were only a few short hours from Aspen. My mind could sense it. I was excited to enter Aspen from a new direction, from its southern entrance, by driving over Independence Pass, a feat not possible by car in the winter. Signs of Colorado's past were ever apparent as we drove past abandoned buildings, ghost towns, and seemingly into the sky. The few other cars on the road were sporadically parked along the way, in each of the coveted spots with the best views.

Ascending for fifteen miles to the 12,095-foot summit of Independence Pass took us from grass, to granite, to dirt, and even to snow. I cannot comprehend how the steep trek was made before automated transportation. The first stagecoach crossed the freshly completed road over Independence Pass in 1881. Yet a lack of roads didn't stop people from following the rumors to Aspen. You may picture Aspen as a town for the rich and famous. While that has definitely not always been the story, it has certainly been the intention.

As it goes with Western towns, in the early days, people went to Aspen for one reason: mining. When Aspen was founded in 1879, under the name of Ute City, it became the destination of those intending to make their fortunes. In 1880, four of Aspen's early inhabitants: Henry P. Cowenhoven, his wife Margaret, his daughter Kelly, and his clerk, D. R. C. Brown, made the trek to Aspen by wagon (over Cottonwood Pass and Taylor Pass, before a road was even built). When the going got rough they unloaded the wagons, packed up the mules, and made do. When the going got really rough, they unloaded the wagons, packed up the mules, disassembled the wagons, lowered them down rock faces by rope, reassembled the wagons, packed them up, and kept moving on. They did this for weeks. It took the party two weeks to go ten miles. I was glad we had a car.

In 1893, only fourteen years after the first explorers made their way over Independence Pass, Aspen had grown to be the third-largest city in Colorado—and in those fourteen years some remarkable things took place. One story caught my eye, because it proved my conviction that *not* everyone who moves to Aspen is a ski bum. A man by the name of Jerome B. Wheeler, a prominent New York business-man, owned 45 percent of the stock of Macy's Department Store in 1879. He became frustrated, as has many an executive with this 45 percent number, because it meant he couldn't control the company as he saw fit. So he said good-bye to the New York corporate world and headed out to Colorado. Wheeler became a part of the Aspen scene when he purchased his first mine in 1882.

So, while it may be true that not everyone who moves to Aspen is a ski bum, I can't dispel the ever-so-popular belief that the rich move to Aspen to live in luxury and to get away from the corporate environment. Jerome Wheeler went on to open the doors to Aspen's first bank in 1884. I guess he had some cash in need of a return. I'm sure he was relieved a year later when Wyatt Earp and a U.S. marshall arrested James Crowthers in Aspen for his Wells Fargo robbery in Arizona. I'm positive the thought crossed Crowther's mind that this booming mining town might also have some money in its bank. Thank God for Wyatt Earp.

When we first sighted Aspen later that afternoon, the city sat in comfort, just as I remembered. We followed Difficult Creek down the steep road into the valley, with glimpses of town and the neighboring meadows at each turn. The road eventually began to level, and we slowly made our way over to Main Street.

As I looked at Justin next to me, memories flashed of the many nights we had dined together with our families after a long day of skiing. I thought about the nights when Justin, Chas, and I ate at Boogie's Diner while our parents dined at the Ute City Bar and Grill. The girls in Mezzaluna also made an appearance in my memory for which I was grateful.

When we passed by the outdoor mall, I had to ask, "Want to run into Curious George's?" I wanted see if George was still sporting his curling mustache that he had worn so proudly, as he walked behind his glass cases of antique guns and knives that we were always eager to see. In short, I was glad to be back.

"No," said Chas, "We'll be back to town in a bit."

We decided to pass through the town and make our way up Castle Creek Road to Eddie and Sherry Wachses' ranch, our new home, in order to unpack and settle in. We had finally made it to our first real resting stop of the trip. As we drove down the driveway, it began to sink in how incredible, and undeserving, the gift was that the Wachses had given us. Although the opportunity to stay at their ranch was the first direct gift that I had received from the couple, my encounters with them in the past had already taught me how amazingly loving and generous the two Chicago natives were. In sincerity, I would have loved it if the two had been there with us the entire time. They guaranteed wonderful company. But I couldn't resist feeling elated that we were going to be spending four days and nights at the ranch on our own. The next summer we were given an even more amazing gift by the Wachses, one that did allow us to spend a great deal of time in their company, also one that you will hear about. But that was unbeknownst to us at the time. We were in serious shock that we were even allowed to spend time at this ranch.

Stunned, we each took our own path through the house for a good ten to fifteen minutes, until it finally began to sink in that we actually got to stay there. Separate rooms would have been possible for all four of us, but we decided to settle into the two bunk rooms so that we didn't abuse our privilege.

As I threw my bag into the corner of the room, I heard Justin yell from across the house, "Hell, yeah! Fridge is stocked with food."

Donald's voice chimed in, "And bronsons!"

Many people would have assumed that the food and beer were not intended for us, but for some reason I knew they were. Chas found the note and read aloud, "I hope you boys made it safely. Here's some food and beer to tide you over. Make yourself at home. Eddie and I wish we could be there to show you a good time. Call us if you need anything. Love, Sherry." Believe me when I tell you that these are amazing people.

You know those feelings that you may get once or twice a year, if you're lucky, when you look around and think about what you're doing and realize that you are in the exact place that you've been dreaming about, essentially living in a dream? Well, surprise, surprise. If you couldn't have guessed, we each had one of those moments that night.

After throwing our steaks on the grill, we each called home to check in (and brag to our parents about what we were up to). Chas had an unexpected conversation.

"What do you mean, I got in?" he asked. "You opened the letter? You serious?"

I exchanged looks with Donald and Justin. We all knew exactly what he was talking about. Chas looked over at me. All he could do was smile. I smiled back, of course.

That phone call marked a dramatic change of events in Chas's life. It marked a change in mine as well. Chas had been accepted to the University of Virginia. He had been on the waiting list, but had not expected to get in. It took me a while to grasp the meaning of the news. On one hand, I had been looking forward to going to Virginia without any close friends. It was my first shot at breaking new ground on my own. But on the other, I was glad to have Chas going with me. Having at least one close friend would make the transition much easier. I quickly embraced the news.

As Chas put the phone down, I walked over and gave him a high five. "Dude, it's going to rock. Congrats, man; I'm pumped!"

Chas couldn't resist a yell. "Hell, yeah!" he said.

The relief in Chas's eyes spread quickly across the room.

"Hey, Houser, pass me a beer," Chas said. "Let's go check on those steaks. Time to celebrate!"

Sitting in the hot tub with cold beers in hand, we were silent as we listened to the ripple of Castle Creek and looked up at the bright stars peering down. The savory taste of our home-cooked New York strips still lingered on our palates. We thought about everything we'd done since leaving Atlanta three short days ago. We also knew that we would be traveling the country over the next three weeks, listening to live music, fly-fishing, mountain biking, and merely enjoying the surprises that came with each new morning. Life didn't get any better than this. We were content, in the utter essence of the word.

Now I would like to expound upon the word *content*. It bothers me when many people mistake the word to mean happy. Happy means that you are enjoying the moment. I can be happy in the crowd at a wedding, yet still be pissed off that I have three exams hanging over my head. I can be happy when I'm at the beach, but still be uncomfortable with sand in my bathing suit.

Content means that not only are you enjoying the moment, but you also would not change a single thing about your situation. You are delighted with where you are, satisfied with where you've been, and are looking forward to what is to come. In moments of contentment you wish the world would stop and take a breather, so you could revel in the moment for eternity. We were content and remained in that mindset for most of our remaining journey. For that reason, I am willing to say that I probably had as good a time on that trip, if you were to add up all of our content moments, as many people have in a year. And I don't mean compared to well-off people, or struggling people, or happy people, or sad people, or open-minded people, or distracted people, or nice people, or jerks. I mean people. We had a good time.

The next morning we decided to reassemble our bikes from their seemingly endless statuelike pose on top of the car. There was a lunch spot that we had been missing. We were anxious to make the eight-mile bike ride to its tables. The four of us rode to the Woody Creek Tavern on the Rio Grande Trail, which follows the Roaring Fork River down the valley below Aspen. After a mid-stroll break to watch the private planes shuffling in and out of the local airport, we dispelled distant thoughts of owning jets and resorted back to the more efficient means of pedaling on down the road. As usual, the burgers at Woody Creek were perfect.

"Ya'll think there are going to be any hotties in Telluride?" Chas asked, as he took a bite.

"Yeah, hotties that don't shave their armpits," laughed Houser.

"Hudson will be in heaven," said Justin.

"Hell, yeah," I broke in, "You got to love hippie chicks."

"Hudson, you're a hippie yourself," said Donald.

"Perhaps," I acknowledged. "I do have a thing for music."

"Chas, your parents were total hippies," said Donald.

"I know," Chas agreed. "They have some damn cool stories, though."

"My dad is the opposite," said Donald, stating the obvious. "An accountant from Georgia Tech."

"My dad went to Tech," said Chas, trying to see if that changed his dad's status.

"Yeah, but didn't he quit school to become a wrangler?" asked Donald.

"Yeah, guess so," replied Chas. "He worked in Texas for a bit on a ranch. Also lived in Canada and built a cabin with his brother."

"Total hippie," said Justin.

Perhaps it was obvious, but we all dreamt of being just like Chas's father—a man of the world who had seen and done it all. Although we were mocking the hippie types, we were also glorifying the concept at the same time. We wouldn't have been on the cross-country excursion that we were on if we hadn't been down-to-earth ourselves. Not that we were out hugging every tree, but we enjoyed the freedom of being on the road and in the mountains.

Aspen has long been a summer destination, for those who realize it, as much as it has been a winter one. The summers may actually be even more enjoyable. The hectic powder can't cast its haunting spell. The activities in the warmer weather offer a broader range of pursuits. In fact, mountain biking, fishing, deep-sea diving, and hiking are all activities that seem to go hand in hand with the place. "Deep-sea diving?" you may ask. "I don't recall there being an ocean nearby." Well, you caught me. Deep-sea diving is far from a common pastime in the area, although I was surprised to discover that it *has* been done before. "Where?" you may ask. "Where in Aspen can you go deep-sea diving?" Where else would crazed and greedy pioneers use a deep-sea diver if problems arose? In a mine.

Aspen's silver mining production fell faster than anyone could have imagined once President Grover Cleveland repealed the Sherman Silver Purchase Act on November 4, 1893. The fact that 80 percent of Aspen's enterprises went bankrupt caused a few folks to be desperate enough to attempt radical measures, such as deep-sea diving in a mine. One such fellow was D. R. C. Brown, whose drastic wagon maneuvers had led him and the Cowenhovens into the city in 1880. Brown's Free Silver Mining Company (and no, he wasn't giving away all the silver) drove a mining shaft that intersected the ores of the Smuggler and the Molly Gibson mines at a depth of fifteen hundred feet. They were delighted to find that silver was there, but with it came a flood of water. To cure the problem, Brown installed new generators for the mine's pumps, but even they couldn't get the last sixty-five feet of water out of the mine.

I don't know how drunk Brown was when he got the idea, or whom he knew to call, but in 1910 he ordered up a few deep-sea divers. The divers came all the way from New York to try to clear any underwater obstructions and get the pumps into working order. The bloody idea worked. Smuggler Mountain released another two million dollars worth of silver ore the next year.

Mining didn't last much longer. If you have to use deep-sea divers to extract silver, you know supply is running thin. What came next? Potatoes. As of 1917, potatoes became the cash crop of the valley. This was not a good sign. The downward spiral had begun. Aspen hit a population low of seven hundred residents in 1930. The town remained in the "quiet years" until Aspen Mountain opened for skiing in the winter of 1947.

When skiing took its first long glide into the city, the locals didn't just sit around and let Aspen Mountain reap all of the rewards. They opened their windows and noticed that there happened to be snow on other mountains as well. Whipple Van Ness Jones—aside from walking around town trying to convince himself that people must be smiling at him because he had graduated from Harvard, and not because they were laughing at his name—also built the Aspen Highlands Ski Mountain in 1957, in order to compete for the profits. Aspen Highlands had the longest vertical drop of any ski resort in Colorado at the time. Because Whipple Van Ness Jones was so fond of his alma mater, he actually donated Aspen Highlands to Harvard in 1993. I can see the headlines now: "Aspen Trades Ski Mountain for Free Culturing to its Hippies." Harvard didn't see much use in owning the mountain. They sold it shortly thereafter.

You may laugh at my imagined headline, but at one point Aspen was indeed in such a state that it considered ridiculous measures to rid itself of hippies. In 1967 the city decided to crack down on the shabby-looking crowd by enforcing an old vagrancy ordinance that prohibited blocking the sidewalk. Basically, it meant if you looked shaggy enough you weren't allowed to sit down. The city magistrate assigned one hippy ninety days in jail and a three-hundred-dollar fine for, yes, sitting on the sidewalk. Les Levine, a renowned contemporary artist in Aspen when the city began its cultural movement, also found himself in the police station for "loitering" around town. I believe he was walking down the street to the grocery store.

At 6:00 AM the next morning I woke up easily, anxious to hit the stream. I talked Justin into waking with me. We headed out the doors toward a place that had been calling my name for months. The two of us drove down the valley to the town of Basalt, then turned in the direction of a certain water that we had heard about. This so-called water happens to be famous.

"Where we headed?" asked Justin.

"Frying Pan River," I said, as I put the car into drive.

"Why's it called the Frying Pan?" Justin was in an inquisitive state.

"You don't even need a rod. I heard the fish just jump right into the pan," I said.

"Damn, think I like this river." He was looking out the window.

As we began to wind our way down valley, Justin spoke again.

"You think you're going to end up back in Atlanta?" Justin asked.

It was shortly after 6:00 AM; I wasn't really ready for all of these questions. But Justin was awake, and that meant I'd better wake up too, because he's not one to sit still.

"Think so," I responded. "Not really sure where else I'd go."

Justin asked, "We still going to live in Colorado at some point?" He turned away from the window and looked over to gauge my reaction. This had been a dream of ours for as long as I can remember.

"Hope so," I said. "Let's move out here for a year after college."

"You're going to finish before I am," he said.

"Shit," I said, in a manner that conveyed that I needed to think it through. Suddenly, it hit me that he was right. "We'll figure it out somehow," I replied after a moment. For the first time, I started to realize that this dream of ours might not be as easy to accomplish as I once thought.

Now, at this point in our lives, we were those kids who showed up to the stream and got on the nerves of the real fisherman. We had no clue what we were doing. To give you a glimpse of our inexperience, let me give you an example. A decent fly-fishing rod and reel will run you about $350 at any Orvis store. We each purchased the whole she-bang at a sporting goods store for about fifty dollars. It's not that the price of the equipment justifies your level of expertise, for we all know people who seem to catch fish with a stick, a piece of rope, and a piece of corn, but in our case, you can go with the price-to-expertise equation.

Justin and I found a spot on the river that wouldn't distract the other fisherman. Well aware of our capabilities, we were not intending to make any enemies before breakfast. We then began to shift the cold tailwater for a golden trout. Justin and I were within shouting distance, but the river, and especially the stretch within my casting reach, began to feel like my own. The rhythm of my casts seemed to match the rhythm of the river. I then cast my way into a rhythm of my own. It was this day that I fell in love with fly-fishing. Don't be mistaken, I did not fall in love with the process of catching fish. Rather, I fell in love with fly-fishing. The first thing you learn when you begin to understand the sport, if you keep an open mind about things, is that there is a serious difference. I didn't catch a single fish that day but left with a passion for the art of it. The feel of the river beneath your feet as you wade out further from obligation is one that forever drives you. All boys want to play in creeks. Fly-fishing is nothing more than an excuse to do so until the day we die.

Although our attempt to feel the bend of the rod proved fruitless that morning, all four of us went back the next day to give it another shot. It was nice to have Donald and Chas with us on the second go-around.

Looking back on it now, it's hilarious how utterly stupid we were about the sport. At one point, Chas called me over to one of his spots because he couldn't figure out what was wrong.

"Paul, put these glasses on, and check this out." He was pointing to a spot about two feet from us, and, lo and behold, there was an actual fish in the river.

Chas continued, "You see him, right? Why can't I catch him? Watch." He was basically holding the line by hand right over the fish's head.

I couldn't figure it out myself. We had a lot to learn. But this learning, if you go about it in the right way, is a process that never ends. You'd be amazed at the lessons you can learn about life as you progress as a fly fisherman. For one, you gain patience. And if you've learned a thing, you'll know that "all we need is just a little patience" (a little tip I picked up from Axl Rose).

3

America's Prettiest Dead End

It was difficult leaving the Wachses' ranch a few days later. We knew we were saying good-bye to comfort. It was like that feeling when you drive away from your old house for the last time. You know it's time to move on, but you wouldn't mind staying a few more days. But the big event was waiting for us in Telluride, and it was time we made our way over. The scenery was beautiful. It actually felt good to be on the road again, watching the landscape change as we wound through the mountains. While each new mile reminded me of what we were leaving, my heart was at ease later that afternoon when we made our final turn toward America's prettiest dead end.

Telluride is geographically poised at the southern end of the Colorado mineral belt, at the base of a collection of large mountains and waterfalls. The Ute Indians were the original residents in the area. They referred to Telluride as the "valley of hanging waterfalls."

Upon arrival, we drove past our campground and went straight into town. We were anxious to look around. We also knew that we would have to stake claim to our camping spot by parking our car in a permanent spot for the festival. We needed to make that thirty-dollar grocery run first. As the pastures began to turn into buildings and I peered left out the window, I noticed the old beaten-up road that my family had taken on a drive to the Smuggler Mine.

The Smuggler was one of the major mines in the area. Telluride didn't mind settling down at the end of the mineral belt. Not only did the town find Aspen's silver, but also gold, lead, and zinc. And as luck would have it, gold became the main treasure. Work was good. Another famous mine, the Tomboy Mine, became one of the world's biggest gold producers. By 1904, over $360 million in gold had been extracted from the area. At the turn of the century, there were more millionaires per capita in Telluride than in New York City. What's up, Aspen? And when you picture rugged old mining towns, you think of rotten wooden structures whose doors are barely hanging on their hinges, right? This is partially true, but when the mines were thriving these places weren't so bad.

Aside from mining, Telluride is also famous for its bank. This bank wasn't special by any means. Perhaps that's why it's famous. The bank is forever remembered, not because of the money that it housed, but for the money which was stolen from it. Butch Cassidy pulled his first heist at the San Miguel National Bank in Telluride in 1889. Butch lived in Ophir, a mining community ten miles south of Telluride. Cassidy walked away with $24,850, none of which was recovered.

After picking up a week's worth of supplies at the grocery store, we cruised back down the valley to our campsite in the town of Illium, seven miles south of Telluride. We were finally ready to set up home for the week to come.

There were only a few other tents set up when we arrived at the campground. We had the privilege of prime picking our week's "throne," which, believe me, is how we felt about the place after seeing what some of the late arrivers had to make do with.

It's interesting watching a festival grow from the beginning. At first you feel as if you're simply at any other campground on the average weekend. Then you start acquiring a few neighbors. You don't really mind, because you've still got your space. But from that point forward, the setting decisively and suddenly changes. What you thought was a space that no one would dare try to squeeze into, three parties fight over. Two eventually compromise and share the spot. Personal space is confined to your sleeping bag. Even then, there's no room in the tent. All four of you have to cuddle up in that baby. Six-man tent, my ass. But slowly you start to become fond of your setup. I'm sure everyone will tell you that they had the best setup at the festival. Well, we did, seriously—except for the RVs; I'll give them that—but don't let them tell you that they camped out at the festival if they were in one of those puppies. Those things are like the Ritz. But, compared to the Ritz, we turned our site into the executive suite at the Hyatt.

We had tarps that covered our entire tent and a good portion of the area in front of the door (our living room). The living room included a card table, four camping chairs (with the cup holders—that is key), a cooler, a stove, a lantern—you name it. We even figured out that if we backed up the car and opened the tailgate, then not only would it elevate the tarps to let the rain drain, but it would also allow the speakers of the stereo to speak clearly to our ears. It was a nice place to hang out.

Telluride is the most classic ski town that I have ever seen. Actually, now that I think about it, the criteria for a ski town nowadays include having a thousand upscale clothing stores, a million tacky T-shirt shops, and a billion rich tourists running around who think they own the place. Telluride doesn't have that. So, I'll say Telluride is the most classic mountain town that I have ever been to. The old bars tease you to have a drink, and the quaint stores tempt your wallet. Once again, we were in the mood for something good to eat (we, at this point, are probably the most particular teenagers in the nation about nice food), and I remembered a spot that my family and I had raved about the previous summer.

Off Main Street, the narrow stairway led us down into the Powderhorn restaurant. A dark, rich atmosphere welcomed our arrival. The hostess walked us past the wooden bar and into the back room. Keep in mind that most of the "festivarians," as they are called at the Telluride festival, were still at the campgrounds stirring up Ramen noodles (we had a stash too) and grilling veggie burritos. The dinner was a huge perk. It also didn't hurt that we had a cute waitress.

"Where are you from?" Chas asked, after she took our order.

"South Africa," she responded, in a beautiful accent.

"I'm going to Kenya in a few weeks," I said, trying my best to make a connection. It was true though; my family was about to take a trip of lifetime.

"Gorgeous country," she said. "You'll have a blast." She didn't seem to fall in love with me upon sight, which was disappointing.

During our meal, I remembered something funny from my previous trip.

"I went on a date here last summer," I said to the group.

"No shit?" said Chas.

"Was that your last one?" asked Donald, in his usual witty manner.

"Probably was, now that I think about it." I wasn't the type to go on a bunch of random dates.

"Who was she?" asked Chas.

"Some girl that took us horseback riding," I responded.

"I told you," said Donald. "She shave her armpits?" We all laughed, as Donald was on a roll.

"Never got that far," I said. "Wish I knew the answer."

"She goes to Vanderbilt," I added. "I was going to set Chas up, but I guess he won't be in Nashville anymore."

The date had been arranged by my mom while our family took the horses out one afternoon. Apparently she thought the girl was cute and managed to organize a date for her son while I was out of hearing range at the back of the pack. Typical mom move.

Back at street level, the lights of Telluride spread an aura resembling a Hollywood set. You had to take a deep breath to soak it all in. We walked down the street on what used to be called Popcorn Alley, due to the constant slamming of the bordellos' doors.

Rumor has it that when the Finnish and Swedish immigrants taught the locals how to ski, it wasn't to show them the joy of skiing, but rather to show the miners how to get down to their favorite bordello faster. So that's what skis are for, huh?

But there were no bordellos to distract our minds. We decided to call it a night and get some sleep, so we could get up the next day and explore. The festival didn't begin for another three days, so we had a couple of days to ourselves. Personally, I was ready to hike around and find some more streams to play in.

When you wake up in a tent, at first you're not sure exactly where the hell you are. Before your mind can catch up to your senses, in that state when you're half-asleep, it comes up with some pretty interesting ideas about where your body might be located. Then come the sounds. The good sound is nothing. And the bad sound, well it's that faint tapping on the nylon that seems to say, "Surprise! You know all of those cool things that you were planning to do today? Nevermore. Nevermore." After you realize what you've woken up to, you will feel your face form expressions of anger that you've never felt about *anything* before. If you were at home, then it would be a great day to go back to sleep for a few hours and then watch movies all day. But you can't do that in a tent. You can't even go back to sleep, because you've woken up in a tent; once you do that, it's all over.

So, what do you do? You sit, wait, sit, wait, sit, talk, sit, wait—this goes on for an hour or two. After that, you sit and wait some more. You finally decide that the rain isn't going to stop you from having fun. You grab a jacket off the ground, mumble something that no one can understand about showing the rain something, and then head out. You're back in five minutes. The jacket gets thrown back on the ground, and you let out some freakish yell that reveals your complete helplessness. Then what do you do? You drink. You might as well. You're not going to drive anywhere. You're not even going to walk anywhere. The bottle has to drain itself sometime, right? Right, and the time is now. We even drank our way back from being miserable to being content.

We were sitting in our throne, cooking up some lunch, sipping on vodka cranberries (I know, we were wimps at the time), listening to CDs of the music we'd be hearing live in two days, laughing with our friends, listening to the rain (aw, who cares anymore ... rain is a good thing ... besides, the grass needed it).

That afternoon we sought to take a rain break by catching a movie in town. Everyone else appeared to have the same idea. It seemed the entire town was packed into the theatre for a few hours of warmth and a ceiling. At first I was a little disappointed that we hadn't escaped the patchouli stench of our neighbors. Then I realized that we *were* inside, and that's all I really needed to know. There was a scene in the movie we were watching where Willie Nelson makes a cameo appearance. The place went up in a roar of cheers. Willie was scheduled to play on opening night. He hadn't played at the Telluride Bluegrass Festival since his first appearance in 1982. I yelled too. I was excited. How could I not be?

It seemed I had been anticipating the start of this Bluegrass Festival every day since the day I first heard about it the summer before. I finally woke up to the morning of the start date. It was June 17, 1999.

4

Telluride Bluegrass Festival

God must like good music. The skies cleared when the first guitars plugged in. A clear sky was only fitting for the setting. The stage lay at the foot of a natural backdrop in the Telluride Town Park, where you were blessed with a view of Bridal Veil Falls as well as the surrounding green of the horseshoed mountains. The contrast of the field's fluorescent tarps, the setting sun, and the grandfatherly steeps was quite a visual, and it will forever last in my memory. Let's just say it was a nice place to hear some good tunes.

Regardless of the cheers God had heard for Willie the day before, Willie must have done something to upset her. Immediate rain accompanied Willie's stage presence. He was the last performer of the night. With the rain, Donald, Chas, and Justin said they'd had enough.

"Come on, Paul," said Chas. "We've heard some good music."

"This rain is miserable," added Donald.

"We're headed back to camp," said Justin, "You ready?"

Hell, no, I wasn't ready. I was ready to hear Willie Nelson. At that point in the trip and at that point in my life, if there was one thing in the world that I wanted to do, besides Cindy Crawford, it was to hear Willie Nelson. I didn't even own a Willie Nelson record, but I loved him. I had probably only heard a few songs, but I loved him for the songs I'd heard. When you know about music, and I like to think that

I do, you know when you're in the midst of it. Willie *was* music. If you thought I cared for one second that it was raining during his performance, then you are sadly mistaken. If anything, it was a nice gesture. The rain cleared the crowd out a little—but only a little. I wasn't the only one in town to see some tunes. It was nice to be there.

The term *bluegrass* comes from the Grand Ole Opry star Bill Monroe's first band, the Blue Grass Boys, which was named after Monroe's home state of Kentucky. From there, almost everything else you need to know about the history of bluegrass is simply that the people who make up its history were on the festival bill.

When the Del McCoury Band and Ricky Skaggs picked the audience to their feet, I could tell in a matter of seconds that they were the real deal. Upon the count of three, the band burst into a two-stepping fury that sprung the crowd from the comfort of their chairs into a jumping sea of laughs and yells. These musicians were the spiritual children of bluegrass's Mother Mary, Bill Monroe, and they knew how to preach to the choir. Del McCoury played with Monroe in the Blue Grass Boys for a year. He moved on to eventually start Del McCoury and the Dixie Pals (can you guess where a few Chicks got the idea for their name?). Del was backed by his two sons, Robbie and Ronnie. Their constant smiles were always complemented by the suits they wouldn't play a note without. If there is one family that knows how to play bluegrass, it is the McCoury boys.

Ricky Skaggs, the other descendent of Mother Monroe, also picked up his skills from the best of the best, and at quite an early age. By his tenth birthday, Ricky had performed with Bill Monroe, Flat and Scruggs, and the Stanley Brothers. He has won four Grammys, although that doesn't set him out as anything special from this Grammy-collecting crowd. As I listened in amazement to his playing, I leaned over and asked someone who he was. The look of disgust that I received threw me off at first, yet I appreciated the look once I understood its intentions.

"Just listen," they replied. "These guys are the backbone of whoever it is you're here to see."

It is true that I knew a lot more about the newer bands on the schedule. Yet part of the reason I came to the festival was to learn about guys like Ricky and Del. I appreciated the disgusted look when I realized its relevance, even though it was ill intentioned.

One of the unique traits of this musical gathering is that the descendents of Monroe perform on the same stage as *their* descendents, who have taken the style to new levels. I was already a fan of one of modern bluegrass's heroes, Bela Fleck. I became an instant fan of another one the second I heard his Dobro's raspy slide.

The artist I'm referring to is a man by the name of Jerry Douglas. Now, this is a guy who will eventually be the next definition in Webster's for the verb *slide*. I honestly wouldn't be surprised to see the entry: "slide (slaid) *v.i.* to move with continuous contact and little friction over a smooth surface/to move quietly and with great ease/ just check out Jerry Douglas if you don't know what we mean." The *New York Times* called him the "Dobro's matchless contemporary master." A Dobro is the type of hollow-bodied guitar you see with that shiny metal face on it. It's great for playing blues, even greater for playing slide, and best when it's in the hands of Douglas himself. Jerry is one of those artists who is so popular in the music world that it would be almost a mathematical surety that you've heard him play before, even if you didn't know it.

While Willie Nelson boasts of creating over one hundred albums, an impressive figure no matter how you cut it, Jerry Douglas has played on more than *one thousand* albums. Now think about this: *one thousand albums!* This guy has probably spent more time recording than he has pissing. He's played on albums by Garth Brooks, Paul Simon, James Taylor, Reba McIntire, Phish—you name it. Many may be surprised to see Phish's name on the list. I assure you, Phish has its bluegrass roots, as much as anyone. I actually had the opportunity to see Phish perform with Ricky Skaggs, Sam Bush, The Del McCoury Band, and Wynona Judd at my first Phish show, in our nation's "country music capital." Wynona Judd sang "Free Bird" as the encore. Pretty cool.

The mainstream crowd has likely heard Douglas play on the song "I Am a Man of Constant Sorrow." Douglas helped put together the *O Brother, Where Art Thou* soundtrack. I think every band at the festival honored Jerry Douglas and Bela Fleck with an invitation to play a few songs. It's not a bad event when you get to listen to the likes of Jerry and Bela at almost every performance.

I've played around with the name Bela Fleck in a manner that assumes instant recognition. You need to feel that he is someone you *should* know. If Jerry Douglas is the master of the Dobro's domain, then Bela Fleck is master of the banjo's. Although fans would like to hear that Bela was an herbivore as a kid, who fed strictly on Kentucky's plains, this man—who is often considered the world's premier banjo player—is in reality a New York City native, regardless of his diet. If we're talking Grammys, you may be interested to hear that he is the only musician who has been nominated for the award in Jazz, Bluegrass, Pop, Country, Spoken Word, Christian, Composition, and World Music. He knows his stuff. And in order to keep up, so must the guys he's got playing next to him. Steve Futterman commented on Bela Fleck and the Flecktones in *Entertainment Weekly*: "Heavyweight players who make an endearing fusion, the Flecktones have a fine time roaming all over the musical map ... it's hard to resist a band that draws on bluegrass, funk, world music, pop, and jazz with such glee and lack of pretension."

Let me give you a little info about Bela's backup band, the Flecktones. They are an interesting breed. Victor Wooten is by far the best bass player that I have ever run across. If you heard him play, you'd know why I say this. Victor Wooten plays the bass like a professor taking a first-grade test. The audience is like a class of elementary school students that can't comprehend the quickness and accuracy of the teacher. We don't know where to even *begin* interpreting the footnotes that reveal the theory behind the formulas. He began learning bass from his older brother at the age of three. Victor made his first professional stage debut when he was five, with the Wooten Brothers Band, which later opened concert tours for Curtis Mayfield. These must have been good training grounds. Another one of the Wooten Brothers still plays right at Vic's side.

RoyEl Wooten, known as Future Man, is a musician, composer, scientist, and inventor. No shit. He plays percussion on the inventions that he creates. You know the guys who you occasionally see on the sidewalk, who play the guitar, drums, harmonica, and God knows what else at the same time, with some creation that they seemed to have picked up from the last guy's trash can? Future Man is their idol. He started off playing his first invention, the *drumitar*, a guitar-shaped instrument that manages to replicate apparently any percussion sound possible. I was shocked at his capabilities on the drumitar, but supposedly it can't touch his new creation: the RoyEl. The RoyEl resembles a keyboard, but is styled after the damn table of periodic elements. I can't wait to see how the hell Future Man uses that one.

The last member of the Flecktones is Jeff Coffin. I'll keep this one simple. Jeff Coffin can play two saxophones at the same time. Well, enough said.

The Flecktones' performance was the first to be graced with a visible, and thankfully spectacular, sunset. When the time felt appropriate, I did one of those moves where you kind of stand up, nod to yourself, and slowly turn in a complete circle to try to capture the moment. Of course, this is never fully possible.

As the sun quickly retreated, I slowly focused more on the music and less on my surroundings. I knew the sun would set again. Although the darkness of night approached with each note, the Flecktones' music brightened up our world. Just as the wind swept the last flickering trace of the sun into the pines, the band lifted our spirits by bringing out a special visitor. Now, if the newcomers bring out Bela Fleck to play, since he is the master of his time, who does Bela bring out as a guest? Tuvan throat-singer Kongor-ol Ondar. Why? Because this guy can sing a three-part harmony with *himself* while picking a damn banjo.

One day, before the festival began, the four of us were walking around town after lunch. I noticed an entranced crowd in a little park off the side of the street. Bela Fleck was just sitting there by himself, playing for whoever wanted to listen. We walked up and stood in admiration for a few minutes, then quickly concluded that, "It's just Bela. We'll see him again," and moved on. That's like walking by Mozart playing the piano in the lobby, and saying, "It's just Mozart. Let's go upstairs and see if the *90210* reruns are on." What can I say? If I had been traveling alone I would have stayed for hours, yet I was there to spend time with my friends too. As I've hinted, they *are* music fans. They are just not quite as fanatical as I am.

Musicianship astonishes me. Great musicians basically step on stage and say, "You see this instrument? I know how it works, and I'm going to show you. Are you ready? Okay, pay attention." It intrigues me that musicians have to take on that level of responsibility. For hours on end, musicians can play long series of notes that the audience wants to hear, and completely hold everyone's attention. This is a difficult thing to do. Think about the service that musicians know how to provide. It is quite valuable. Musicians take entire rooms full of people away from their worries and into pleasant states of mind. Thousands of stressed people—people stressed about work, people stressed about relationships, people stressed about life—all walk into a performance from separate directions. In an instant, people unite, stress disappears, and hidden smiles emerge. Good moods are created out of thin air. When all is said and done, the people in the crowd walk back to their cars—changed, happy. Everyone simply feels a little better than they did only hours before. Music can refresh an unlimited number of people simultaneously. That, to me, is simply incredible. Music approaches religion. Often, music *is* religion.

Now, I can only imagine what it would be like to perform for thousands and thousands of people. Yet, I will say that I have an idea. You see, playing live music is merely one step better than simply playing music. It can be a tall step if things go well. But I've had practices at which everything just clicked, and I had a better time when that happened than at performances in front of sold-out rooms. What makes for better nights than others is communication: communication within the band, and communication with the audience. With-out communication, whether you are at a practice in your parents' basement or in front of relentless screaming voices, it will feel like a piece of the music is missing. Because I have felt strong musical com-munication, even though this may have been in a basement or may have been in a bar, I honestly *do* feel that I know what it would be like to play for thousands of people. With music, it doesn't matter where you are; if things are on, then things are on, and that feeling can hap-pen anywhere.

In a sense, strong musical communication actually feels a little telepathic. When things go well, you seem to read the minds of the other people who you are playing with. During a performance, you are constantly asking yourself, "Where do we go from here?" If every-one is not aware of the answer then you have a communication break-down. The music falls apart. But if everyone knows the proper direction, the music works. Sometimes this sense of direction requires acute instincts. Other times it requires preparation. The unspoken dialogue usually requires a little of both. No matter how you find communication, you've got to make sure you arrive there. A band has to be trucking down the highway at the same speed, in the proper direction, in order to discover unknown roads. You can't navigate these roads unless you communicate.

A few days later, the festival was gone—passed by in a flash. After the final song, a difficult moment to bear, the stage fell silent. The PA system began to play recorded songs of the past. We reluctantly headed back to our throne in Illium, sad that our fortress would be destroyed in a matter of hours. Throughout the deadness of the night, we heard yells of "Festivaaaaaaal!" from far and wide. The warmth of a nearby fire invited us to sit with our neighbors and talk above the yellow flame. We listened to stories about how each of our neighbors reunited year after year for the annual event to reestablish their right-ful territory and feast on the pleasures of the music and companionship.

Musical experiences constantly drive me. Not a day goes by in which music is not a part. If I'm in the car, the stereo is on. If I am at home, I am either behind my keyboard or serving as the resting stop for my guitar strap. I was sad that the Bluegrass Festival was over. Thankfully, this was not the end of my trip. It was for Chas. His cousin was getting married and Chas had to fly out the next day to be with his family (the only excuse I would have taken, but a great one at that). Donald, Justin, and I were to finish up our journey one man short.

"We'll see you back in Atlanta," I said to Chas, as I shook his hand.

"Wish I could stay," he replied. "Hard to leave Colorado."

"Gets harder every time," I said.

"Yeah," he replied with a nod. "Gets harder every time."

5

Moab Desert

Everyone has their favorite drives—to each their own curves in the road that lead them to peaceful memories. The best drives may be those that we have only seen once in a lifetime, but that we will forever remember. I'm using the word *drive,* instead of the word *roads,* because it is not the roads that cast a spell on us. Rather, it tends to be the landscape that the roads lead us through that we remember. I got to drive one of those drives the day we left Telluride. As we rolled out of town, with the previous week already in our rearview mirror, we headed west on Highway 145 toward the imaginary line between Colorado and Utah.

This line turns out to be not very imaginary. You begin the drive in the San Juan Valley, with tall green mountains in every direction. As the miles add on to your odometer, the mountains eventually taper off to decisive plateaus. With each turn you seem to find yourself in a different valley. Then the greens turn to purples, and the purples suddenly turn to red. When the red part happens, you know you are in Utah. The southeastern ridge of Utah's border is protected by the La Sal Mountains. Beyond that, Utah was red, dry, and flat.

Our eyes were confused at first and had to adjust to the earth's new look. I was excited, though. The new look meant new terrain to explore. The arid Utah desert we drove through was home to a little town named Moab. This little town was the home of the desert's best mountain-biking trail. We were glad *our* trail led us to its beginning.

Moab's beginning did not, as our other towns had, result from any great discovery of minerals. Aside from the Utes, once again, the original inhabitants, the Spanish explorers were the first to discover the area. In fact, the Old Spanish Trail, which connected Santa Fe to Los Angeles (not in the most direct route, to say the least), went right through the Moab area. Years later, under the direction of Brigham Young and other Mormon leaders, twelve men set out to establish a major control point on the Spanish Trail. They were successful. The next year, in 1855, forty-one men were called by the Mormon Church to set up the Elk Mountain Mission where Moab stands today. This first settlement did not last long. Only one month later, a battle took place between the local Utes and the Mormon settlers. Two missionary hunters were killed. The group decided to abandon the mission. The first permanent residents didn't come back to Moab until 1878 (and then more to farm than to pray).

Moab has had a fluctuating economy ever since. A variety of factors have been the cause of this. The town's economy was originally based on farming, ranching, and fruit growing. This is much less exciting than gold, I know. The locals thought so as well. Yet mining did come into play down the road. While nobody found their fair share of silver or gold, miners discovered a much more powerful substance: a rich deposit of uranium. Uranium is the dangerous stuff that nuclear bombs rely on. The Moab economy of the 1950s hinged on the uranium boom, during the Cold War that was driven by the arms race between the United States and the Soviet Union. Once that died down, oil, another wartime substance, drove the economy until wells ran dry.

The current economy has favored peace more than controversy. Moab's supply-and-demand chart has recently been driven by tourism. In a sense, tourism was the reason we drove into town, although we considered ourselves cyclists much more than tourists.

It is only fitting that we escaped to this land of prehistoric desolation after visiting Telluride. Butch Cassidy had the same idea after he robbed the San Miguel National Bank. Fleeing from the scene, Butch boarded the Moab ferry by force and took it across the Colorado River, to get away from any pissed-off cohorts with less-than-full pockets.

Butch Cassidy, Harry Longabaugh, and the rest of the Wild Bunch would use the Moab area to hide out after many of their infamous robberies. In case you're curious, Harry Longabaugh, a.k.a. the Sundance Kid, achieved his nickname by spending two years of jail time in Sundance, Wyoming, for stealing cattle. He was not part of the Telluride robbery, but joined the group for most of the Wild Bunch's later escapades. I feel I must give a quick, and I do mean unjustly quick, recounting of the Wild Bunch's story. I could not appropriately write about the West without giving them their due credit for terrorizing it.

After the Telluride robbery, Butch's mischievous buddies enjoyed their new outlaw roles so much that they decided to keep up the profession. While Butch took a sabbatical to relish his share, the others took the liberty to rob the Wallowa National Bank in Enterprise, Oregon, and a bank in Delta, Colorado. Yet Butch couldn't stay either honest or bored for long. He wound up doing a year and a half in the Wyoming State Prison after being caught with a stolen herd of horses. With his time in prison, Butch had quite a few nights to plan his future life of pure and healthy theft. So once he found himself on the other side of the bars, Butch formed the band of robbers that later became known as, among many names, the Wild Bunch. This gang consisted of about fifteen greedy souls (occasionally including a few prostitutes who rode along to join in some of the fun).

Their first job together was a bank in Montpelier, Idaho, in 1896. Now, for some reason, when I pictured Western outlaws, I thought about them riding from town to town to stay one step ahead of the last town's sheriff. But apparently, at least for this bunch, they knew how to get around. Over the next few years they robbed a bank in South Dakota, the Overland Flyer train in Wyoming, a bank in Nevada, and the Northern Pacific train in Montana. And they wouldn't just head into the local mountains to hide out after each robbery, either. They would head to Texas or Moab or Wyoming. It appears that they knew how to get away. But once Harry and Butch decided that their footprints were a little too visible, they took off to South America to lie low. As I implied, we usually think that people in the Old West didn't get around much, but the railroads weren't in place just to ship cargo. Butch Cassidy and the Sundance Kid took a train to New York City in order to catch the next departing international ferry.

Cassidy and Sundance found themselves sailing from New York to Buenos Aires, intending to avoid the rotten food they remembered in the U.S. penitentiaries. They actually worked for an honest living on a ranch in Argentina for a couple of years. But once you become a great robber you tend to do what you know best. The chain of plundered banks they visited in South America is almost equally as impressive as those they left behind up North. But as we all know, at least all of us who have seen decent movies, their story does not have a happy ending. After *borrowing* some of the silver from the Chocaya Tin-Silver Mine in Bolivia, instead of finding themselves on a safe getaway, they found themselves surrounded by the Bolivian army. Except for a few who proclaim that Butch Cassidy, the Sundance Kid, Elvis, and Tupac all managed to make it to a deserted island, surrounded by beautiful women, most consider this the end of the tale. Although their ending was tragic, their legacy will surely live on. What good is the West without Butch Cassidy and the Sundance Kid?

We were also thrill seekers when we made our way to Moab. Granted, this was on a different scale, but dangerous nonetheless. The mountain biking in Moab is synonymous with the word treacherous. When we arrived, the heat was blinding. The thought of biking in that weather did not come naturally. In order to prepare for our ride, we needed rest. We made our way straight to the Arches National Park, eighteen miles outside of Moab, to set up camp and rest for the next day's ride.

Arches is best known, as its name implies, for natural rock arches scattered throughout the park. You've probably seen one on the Utah license plate. These arches leave tourists, nature lovers, and nature-loving tourists gaping through handspringing pieces of solid earth. They resemble a variety of gravity-defying formations and appear to be close cousins to extraterrestrial bridges and the original architectural blueprint for the Arc de Triomphe. Most people don't really get excited when they see rocks, but if God had a pet rock, it would be in this place. The park seems to be the world's first Stonehenge.

The pleasures are not limited to daylight. Have you ever seen the stars before? I mean, have you ever *really* seen the stars? I realized that night that I was probably looking up at about ten times as many stars as I had ever seen in a night. I'm talking star*light,* star*bright* here. I wished everyone I knew could take a good look at the twinkling panning lenses that swept across our sky—not a bad place to camp out.

"That the Big Dipper?" asked Donald, pointing in the wrong direction.

"Come on, Houser," said Justin. "It's over there."

"This place is unreal," I said.

"I'm not so sure about Atlanta," Justin remarked. "It'd be nice to see the stars more."

"It'd be nice to have a bed instead of lying in the desert," said Donald.

"I'll trade a bed for this view," I responded.

"I wish we had some chicks out here," Donald chimed in. "Not much fun with you dudes."

"When do you think you'll get married?" Justin asked, after a few minutes of silence.

"Married?" I asked. "I better find a girlfriend first. From the looks of it, I ain't getting married anytime soon."

"I'll probably meet a hottie at Georgia," said Donald. "I'll bet I'm married before I'm thirty."

"I'm not sure if I'm ever getting married," said Justin.

"Rainer, your mom would kill you," said Donald truthfully.

"I know, but how do you know when you found the right one?" he asked.

"I think we'll just know," I said. "At least that's what they say."

"I don't know about married," Donald laughed. "But if we had some girls out here we might end up with some babies!" which cracked us all up. After that, not much else was said and we dozed off, laughing at the world.

We woke up in a different mood. This time it was not the rain that bothered us. The torture came from the sun. At the crack of dawn, the sun was so hot that we woke up in baths of our own sweat. I turned my head to see Donald slowly sit up and look around. His eyes were painfully awake. He didn't have to mutter a word to express his displeasure. Donald's disheveled appearance caused my own uncomfortable frown to rise, slightly, but it quickly receded with the next bead of sweat.

Justin was also aware of the situation. "What the hell? Why *are* we in the damn desert?"

Donald eagerly jumped in, "Fuck this. I'm going to a hotel."

Now, I'm not opposed to roughing it. But I am opposed to misery. We sure as hell were not going to sit there all morning with our skin cooking itself for breakfast. That was for damn sure. *Hotel, here we come.*

The drive back toward town was an easy one to make. Give us tourism, give us motels, give us air-conditioning—just give us *cool*. We made our car a human refrigerator. That didn't do the trick. When you're that hot, no matter how cold the air is, your throat remembers your pain. We needed something cold to drink, and fast. We got some weird looks at breakfast for guzzling our water faster than they could pour it. Our waitress came by with a look of confused concern. "Here you go," she said, handing us a pitcher. "You boys might want this."

As it turns out, not only did we want it, and not only did we need it, but we really should have bought about ten bottles to store it for later that afternoon. You see, that bike ride I told you about was in the middle of the freaking desert too.

The Slickrock Bike Trail, the luring, treacherous path that brought us here, becomes even more dangerous than its natural state once bikers like us show up with about as much water as you need to get from the parking lot to the trail. And we had even anticipated the need for additional water and brought an extra bottle or two. We didn't need an extra bottle or two. That's like thinking one more chip will satisfy you when you know you're going to need the whole bag. We needed *coolers* of it. We were rationing water like we were the modern Three Amigos. We basically *were* the damn Three Amigos. We were that naïve about what we were getting into.

The trail was dubbed the Slickrock Trail, since the early settlers' metal-shod horses had not found it easy to cross the looming expanses of rock. This may not sound very appealing to ride a bike across either. That's the secret. It turns out that rubber loves the naked sandstone. You can ride across it as if it were sandpaper. The traction created between the tires and the rock even allows you to bike up steep slopes that you wouldn't even think you could climb up with your hands. Moab is a very cool place to mountain bike. If we had had enough water we would have stayed all day.

The trail crossed flat plateaus, dove down incredible steeps, wound around boulders, and unfortunately put us *on belay* to grind back up. Although it was a shorter visit than we would have liked, we were fully appreciative of the experience. As we climbed back toward the car, Justin looked back and suddenly told us to stop. "Turn around," he said. I turned back to discover a breathtaking view of the vast expanse of terrain we had just traversed. And right in the middle of my vision stood an immense boulder, sitting in reverie.

Justin sized up the boulder and then shot me a quick glance.

"Are you thinking what I'm thinking?" he said.

My response? An understanding nod, followed by a simple, "Yeah."

Justin shares the taste for good photography that I do. Somehow he knew that I would immediately understand the necessity of taking a picture on top of the boulder. I didn't even think we could climb the thing, but I knew Justin would find a way. We each took turns posing on the proud piece of rock, attempting to steal a piece of its glory. As I rotated my body for the pleasure of my eyes, I had one of those moments in which I realized that I was living a dream.

There are places in your imagination that compose your own photo album, which is forever engraved Life's Checklist. If we find our way to view them, and I mean if we *ever* find our way, then our lives come one step closer to fulfilling their potential. I made a mark on my list that day. All of my conversations about Moab, and the stories I'd heard about it, could now be placed in the category labeled, "I know—I've been there."

We drove out of Moab the next day—with a little more sleep under our belts after a night in the hotel room—but also with a lot more pride. You may say pride should only result from acts of honor and from acts of unselfishness. Yet I say pride should also come from wisdom. When you have visited a place that was held in your heart by the thoughts that brought you there, you have become a wiser person. I was proud that I had checked off a part of a very long list. I now understood Moab. I had now *been to* Moab. No one could take that from me. Think about the conversations you've had wherein people describe a distant place that they've been to. Think about the times when someone else has listened to their story and responded, "I know. I've been there." The gloating storyteller's edge is gone, their story shattered. That's power. Whether you realize it or not, the more you travel, the more powerful you become—and with this power comes wisdom, but it is not a false wisdom imagined *through* power. The power *comes from* the wisdom.

In a sense, the drive out of Moab was the end of our trip. We drove out of Moab with full hearts and content minds. The rest of the trip was more a time of reflection than it was a time of new achievements.

The road we now followed made its way down to Santa Fe, New Mexico. After spending weeks traveling between mining towns and the desert, I was glad to drive back into a decent-sized city, comparatively speaking. There was a basic busyness that welcomed us back to a little more of the real world.

We quickly discovered that Santa Fe was not such an exciting place for eager teenagers to visit. In fact, there was so little for people our age to do that we even talked ourselves into getting excited about the things our parents would want us to do. We walked amongst the downtown shops. We admired the Native American jewelry. We even visited the Georgia O'Keeffe art museum. Aren't you proud? I'm not as much proud as I am glad that there was an air-conditioned building in the area. As I mentioned, we didn't really mind that there wasn't much to do, because we were visiting the town with our minds trapped in the previous day's adventures. They stayed that way all the way home.

It's a weird feeling when you're on the way home from a much-anticipated trip. Not only can you not believe that it is ending, but you also can't believe that you did it. It's sad in a way, but it is a sadness that results from happiness. And it's not really sadness, even though it feels that way. It's more of an understanding of accomplishment, coupled with a realization that you must return to normality in order to prepare for the next trip. The next trip, unfortunately, must usually occur after your mind forgets why you love traveling so much. You'd like to stay on your trip forever. That's just not realistic. You need to get back into the routine of life, begin to remember the pains of the routine, and then dread the pains of the routine so much that you are ready to take off again and relearn why escape can be so truly wonderful.

What's sad to me is the notion that extended travel would not necessarily result in extended joy. Your mind would forget what it is that you love so much about the escape. It's sad that it takes realizing why you want to get away to make a trip as enjoyable as possible. It'd be nice if you could just take off for good, with those you love, and remember forever why it is you are traveling, without a single hint of the feeling fading. I am not sure whether this is possible. There are ties in your daily life that bring you back home. I'd actually be cautious of those who could travel continuously. It would mean to me that they don't have as much to love at home. The key is keeping it all in balance, which is a very personal thing.

We drove home, taking a nap in Memphis, crossing fourteen hundred miles in two days. When we took off three weeks earlier, we had an idea of what would take place. We had no idea about how it would feel. With the windows down and the sun shining over us, we drove across a new part of the nation, as we reflected on that feeling. And then, as if we had never left, we walked back into our homes.

When I opened the door and heard the normalcy of the actions taking place, I would have loved to simply listen for hours. As you know, that can't happen. You miss the faces and they miss yours.

"Paul, is that you?" said my mom, as I cracked the door. She was beaming when she walked into sight. Immediately, I felt glad to be home.

As my parents would tell you, the smile could not be wiped off my face. Our family sat for dinner as one, elated to have each other's company. Of course, my family was as happy as I was about my trip.

I began to tell the story. The words seemed to lose their way—words lost in the air. I could tell that the only thing my family paid any attention to was the look on my face as I was talking. My words couldn't express the trip. My smile could. Yet I didn't want the words to be lost forever. I still wanted those words to reach them. I'm glad I figured out the way.

6

Ol Malo, Kenya

Departing home is perhaps the single most important aspect of growing up. How can you claim to know the world if, in fact, you've never seen it? Whether you move to a new city for a few years, attend college in a different part of the country, or simply get in your car and begin taking trips, it is crucial to meet new people and see new places. You need to take steps to view the world's broader scope. Many people often forget that the mere act of being born in a city does not necessarily preclude other cities having redeeming qualities.

Our trip across the country enlightened me. Atlanta's skyline has new meaning now that I have walked in the plains of Kansas. Georgia's Smokey Mountains invoke new perspective when I compare them to the Rockies. I'll say it again: everyone should drive across the country with friends. I can't contemplate a regret that such a trip could create. You need to see a thousand different cities before you begin to understand even one of them. The world has its patterns and its mechanisms. You need to travel to discover the links in the chain.

Traveling abroad is even more crucial than domestic travel. When you travel in a foreign country the lessons will be in subjects you've never taken. A trip across the United States can take you from algebra to calculus. A trip to Spain is, well, a lesson in Spanish. You need both. What good is a mathematician if he can't communicate?

A month after traversing the United States I found myself standing in Europe—Zurich to be exact. It's not often that you have a glass of chardonnay with lunch. Yet, if you are sitting on the patio of a gorgeous hotel watching boaters motor out of calm canals and into a mighty lake, a glass of chardonnay begins to make much more sense. This is especially true when you begin to take notice of the greater setting. Historic banks, hotels, and apartments line the metropolitan streets. There are no skyscrapers. The majority of the buildings are no taller than ten stories. But the buildings' artistic and historic appearances are as finely tuned as the buildings of Paris. Yet in contrast to most cities you are now envisioning, the wave of commercial activity ends abruptly at the edge of crystal blue water. You could spend the morning in UBS Warburg and eat lunch on your sailboat. If you took the afternoon off, you could even head up into the hills and see a little snow. Quaint towns grace the banks of the lake. As we gazed out across the water and up into the spiraling mountains, it was not a distant notion that Zurich was the mighty center of Europe.

"It's great to be with you kids," said my father during lunch. "I love having the family together."

"Look at the lake," said my mom, in awe. We were seated on the patio of Hotel Baur Du Lac, which had an extraordinary view.

"This menu is too fancy," said my sister Taylor, exhausted from the flight. "I don't even know what this stuff means."

"I'm sure they have something basic," said my mom. "Just ask for the chicken."

"When do we leave again?" asked Taylor, comforted after she did notice chicken on the menu.

"Tomorrow morning," said Dad. "We've got another long flight."

It was such a shame that we didn't have more time to spend walking the streets and enjoying the city. One of the things I love most about Europe is that you constantly find yourself on foot. As you work your way through the maze of streets, you discover the hidden cafés. As you round each corner, you uncover new perspectives and unique settings. This is harder to achieve in a car. When driving, we tend to take the routes we know best; we seek the known, not the new. So I was disheartened that Zurich was only a European power nap. Just when my shoes began to embrace the cobblestones, they walked off the sidewalk and back onto a plane. If you were looking forward to a story about Europe, it will come later, but not now. There aren't many streets where I'm taking you next.

Only a day after descending into the rolling green hills outside of Zurich, Mom, Dad, Taylor, and I were back at the airport, ready to depart. We flew direct from Switzerland to Nairobi, Kenya. After a short drive and a hurried breakfast, our family crammed into a bush plane and made a quick hour's jump to our first destination. In only two days I'd had meals in the United States, Europe, and now Africa. Not too shabby for a weekend excursion.

Our hosts, Rocky and Colin Francombe, arrived in their jeep just as our plane touched down onto a bumpy dirt strip, not three hundred yards from their doorstep. Colin stood tall in his faded green shorts and matching shirt. Rocky wore khaki, a white top, and a large, tan hat. Even as we taxied toward their jeep, it was blatantly apparent that they were an enthusiastic couple. Both were waving and smiling relentlessly. Gauging their actions you would've thought we were their children returning home from war, or that they at least knew us!

I stepped out of the plane as the engine died down. Colin grabbed the bag out of my hands and threw it up on his shoulder. "Welcome to Africa," he said. His grin grew even larger.

The fact that I was actually standing in that particular spot seemed far from reality. Our reception mirrored that of close friends, even as we said hellos. Within one minute our bags were in the back of the jeep, and we were dusting down the path toward their home. Apparently, we were late. I didn't think you could be late for anything in the depths of Africa. We managed to do it.

Holding her hat from the wind, Rocky turned around from the front seat to explain.

"We've got a surprise for you. Sorry to rush, but you came here to see animals, right?"

Walking through their doorway felt like walking into the cover of *Travel and Leisure*. My father was too dumbfounded to speak. I could see my mother's eyes light up like candles. The Francombe estate has a name of course: *Ol Malo,* or *Place of the Greater Kudu.* Their humble abode is a five-thousand-acre ranch and game sanctuary. The Francombe home and sister cottages consist of an elaborate system of natural stone and thatch that, although subtle, may be the nicest place you've ever been.

Yet before we could mutter a word, we were quickly escorted out back, directly to the edge of a landlocked bluff. A lone telescope stood in the yard as if it marked an *X* on a sandy island.

"Take a look," Colin remarked, as he placed our bags into the grass.

As the blurred vision slowly began to clear, I peered closer, with quite eager concentration.

"Great timing," Colin remarked. "We don't see these too often. They tend to hide out." *What,* I am wondering at this point, *is so special about a bunch of branches and leaves?* I was staring at pure brush. *I came all the way here to see this?*

I looked harder. As the telescope kept its secret in hiding, I couldn't help but wonder if the lenses would eventually decide to show me the prize, or if they would continue in childish selfishness forever. My patience hadn't yet adjusted with the setting, but all of my anxiety subsided rather quickly when I saw the animal sitting peacefully in the shade.

"You see him?" Colin remarked. He was beaming.

"Yeah," I exclaimed, my eye squinting deeply into the lens. "Pretty cool."

The leopard sat unaware of our intrusion, only about a hundred yards from the base of the Francombes' estate. We had a bird's-eye view on our prey, as we stood atop massive cliffs, which I must say helped a good bit.

"He made a kill yesterday," said Rocky. "He's been here ever since. Take a good look at him now. I doubt he'll be back after nightfall."

You know you're in a good place when people refer to night as "nightfall."

It was July 4, 1999. I find it ironic that we were celebrating the concept of our American independence on such a vast landscape, which had only barely been tamed, threatened, or controlled. *This power was not gained through wisdom on a visit.* Africa's supremacy was born at the beginning of time, before visitors arrived. You must go there to feel it—and keep your eyes open.

Later that afternoon, Colin was guiding us through the rugged brush on our first day's tour. He sat atop his camel like a cowboy sitting on his horse: comfortable and experienced. The fifth pack of zebras in that hour ran briskly beside us. Colin watched them pass as if they were his friendly neighbors.

"How long have you lived here?" asked Taylor, as we stopped for a break in the tour.

"I grew up in Kenya," said Colin. "Pretty different from the States, huh?"

"Do you ever get bored?" Taylor asked in a naïve tone.

"Oh, Taylor," said my mom, as she looked over at Colin. "She's used to city, I guess."

"No, never bored," said Colin, in honest response to the question. "In fact, quite the opposite." As he said this, a giraffe walked into view and began nibbling on a branch.

Then the unthinkable happened.

Colin told us, with much regret, that it was time to turn around to head back to the house. We rounded a corner, expecting a view of the path back home—not so. Instead, we saw quite the dramatic sight. Sitting in the grass was a candlelit dinner table dressed in bright white and silver. Surrounding the table were low-hanging trees with branches that appeared to be giraffes bending down to feed. People were milling. Glasses were paired with wine. The smell of a burning fire was near. We were too astonished to speak. The camels walked into the perfect natural dining room and lowered us down to our seats.

"I guess this isn't so boring," said Taylor, who had begun to appreciate the surroundings.

This is the reason you go to Africa. This is the reason you travel, period—to have experiences otherwise considered impossible. Many people fear travel because of the uncertain nature of a trip. So many things can go wrong. So many details sound too hard to organize. Yet once you gather the courage to depart, you learn to embrace the uncertainty. Uncertainties are where the rewards lie.

The second surprise was even more chilling than the first. Sitting at this table of kings within the forest were none other than my aunt, uncle, and two cousins. Now, we knew they were at Ol Malo. The Carters had been in Africa for two weeks on a journey of their own. Their last stop of the trip was our first. This was not a coincidence, but rather a miraculous job of planning. We just didn't expect to find them waiting to join us for dinner in a setting of such unique perfection.

What a way to celebrate Independence Day! The holiday is one of the few days when we as Americans focus more on the essential tradition of gathering together as a family. This one took the cake. There had been Fourth of Julys with the Carters in Florida—but to celebrate the occasion in the plains of Africa—at a table for ten, with zebra and giraffe grazing in the distance? I'm searching for the words to describe the overwhelming event and am coming up drastically short. It was a breathtaking night, I assure you.

Together, our families were eight. Taylor and I sat downwind, across from our cousins Palmer and Benjamin. Mom and Dad huddled with Aunt Tricia and Uncle Ben at the upper end of the table. Then Rocky and Colin took to the heads of the table. They sat like worn encyclopedias at the ends of a bookshelf—our knowledgeable bookends keeping us in order.

The feast was like Thanksgiving, taken to a new level. The experience was almost too surreal for speech, but not for long. Once we poured the last drop of red wine, Rocky revealed a hidden magnum of champagne. Aha! The night was young. Once the champagne was opened, the stories spread like wildfire. The Carters' stories always fare better than most. These were of novel rank.

"Now, how often do you have dinner like this?" Tricia asked Rocky, envious of the idea.

"Oh, every few weeks," she said. "We like to surprise our new guests this way."

"Not a bad life," said Ben. "You kids should appreciate this."

"I'd appreciate some more wine!" said Benjamin, laughing.

"Ya'll, I just can't believe we are out here!" said my aunt, still dumbfounded.

"You Hudsons have quite the trip coming up," Ben said. We were about to visit the places they had gone, in reverse order.

"You said you saw lions?" Taylor asked Benjamin.

"Yeah, we even saw a lion kill," my cousin Palmer replied, almost laughing at the absurdity of it.

"Were you close?" my mom said, shocked and worried about what we might encounter.

"Almost had my arm chopped off," laughed Ben. In reality, they had seen the kill from afar.

Now, I hope you don't mind me bragging about our hosts. The Francombes will always please my memory. Their smiles and enthusiasm embraced us at first sight, and continued to do so until we parted. Their smiles are reassuring, especially given that they have not always lived an easy, comfortable life. You see, living in Kenya presents itself with troubles we can't imagine.

"Forgive me if I've been quiet," said Colin, as the dinner was winding down. "Three weeks go we had a tragic loss—we lost our head guide."

At that point, he had our utmost attention. We sat in wonder, eager to learn more.

"What happened?" asked Taylor.

"He was gored to death," said Rocky, "by a water buffalo."

There was silence. No one knew what to say. *Gored to death by a water buffalo?* We weren't in Kansas anymore—that was for sure.

"He had been with us for many years," said Colin. "A true friend."

The water buffalo are some of the most dangerous animals in Africa. Encountering a rogue one is not usually a pleasant occurrence. Water buffalo travel in packs of females that are led by a lone male. This, of course, angers the other males a great deal—so much so that they travel alone. From time to time, another male will challenge the lead male to a duel, just as any sane man would. But if you come upon a deserted male, a rogue male, you can be assured that he is not in the best of moods, for obvious reasons. You can't blame him, but they are dangerous as hell.

"Colin tracked down the buffalo a few days ago," said Rocky. "And killed him."

"An old custom," said Colin. "Can't let the wild get the better of you."

"It is important for the locals to seek revenge," said Rocky.

"It was important to me, honey." said Colin, as he looked at Rocky.

The way that Colin described the loss of the guide assured me that the man had not been just a guide, but rather an intimate part of their family.

To give you a better idea about Colin, the girls that he protects, and the place he's forced to protect them in, I will tell you that this was not the first time he has had to perform the ritual. Life is a delicate thing in Africa.

I had no idea at the time, but Colin and Rocky had already made a name for themselves. It surprises me very little that the family is, in fact, quite renowned. They are remembered for their dedication to the country, their perseverance through hard times, their passion for conservation, and, I'm sure, mostly for their loving friendship and compassion.

Kuki Gallman tells part of the Francombes' story in her novel *I Dreamed of Africa* (you may have seen the book's movie if you're a Kim Basinger fan). While I can't share all of the stories, (the Francombes are what you would call main characters in Kuki's account), I would like to provide a passage. If you're reading this book to get something truly meaningful out of it, I would like to strongly recommend that you read *I Dreamed of Africa*. It will take you away from my story and focus on another, but, I assure you, the other offers many more lessons. You will also undoubtedly appreciate the setting of my story that much more.

Kuki remembers, "They were a happy couple. Rocky was redheaded, with hazel eyes and freckles; slim, tall, and extremely efficient. She came from a family of pioneers and farmers. During the war her father had commanded a column of Chindits in Burma under General Wingate, and, as a result of his bravery, had become one of the youngest brigadiers in the British Army; he was known as 'the happy brigadier.' Colin was tall, good-looking and good-natured, with an open smile of white, even teeth; he was capable, and very much in charge, self-assured, and dedicated to the ranch and its wildlife. His father had been a wing commander in the Royal Air Force, who had retired to Kenya after the war. When King George VI died, Princess Elizabeth was visiting Kenya with her husband, the Duke of Edinburgh. Colin's father was given the task of flying the new queen from Nairobi to Entebbe, from where she proceeded to England; he was the first person in history to pilot an aircraft carrying an English queen. It was clear that both Colin and Rocky loved the place. They welcomed us with their warmth and hospitality, which I came to know well in the years to come."

That night, it was only fitting that the shooting stars stopped by our galaxy for a brief moment before heading out into eternity. I have mentioned that the night sky in the desert of Utah was larger and brighter than any I'd ever seen. The Kenyan sky was far more jaw dropping.

At first it was only the cousins who lay by the pool, letting dinner's spirits carry our enthusiasm longer than we should have. Taylor and I had spent many nights with our cousins, particularly at the beach in Ponte Vedra and at the farm in Madison, enjoying our time in a Carterly fashion. It was simply good to be back in their company—too good for our parents' liking. As our voices echoed and chased the stars, my aunt stormed out of her villa, yelling, "Go to bed!" She appeared pissed. We laughed off her anger, because we all knew she wasn't really mad. If you knew my aunt well, you would immediately realize that she was far from irritated. She was jealous, more than anything, that we seemed to be having more fun than she was at that point in the night.

"Mom, chill out!" Benjamin barked back. "You're louder than we are! We're just looking at the stars."

She eagerly looked up. "Wow," she accidentally whispered out loud. "They're huge."

My aunt is a child at heart, and she quickly let her knees give way, as she knelt down beside us to gaze out in awe. We must have stayed there for hours—not a bad way to end my first day on the continent.

My feeling of contentment hit me again the following morning. The Carters' plane buzzed the house and tipped its wings, as they took off back to Atlanta. At the time, we were driving out to admire the animals grazing on a nearby hill.

When we returned for lunch, I looked forward to another chance to simply sit and eat with Rocky and Colin. Our family was tired from the travel. If left alone, we would have been still and quiet. But the couple's energy revived us. Colin sat down and folded his hands on the table, as if we were about to discuss something of grave importance.

"How'd you like that drive?" he asked. "Amazing, huh?" He was laughing to himself and shaking his head. I guess I was right. This *was* an essential talk.

"Never gets old," Colin added. "This is a gorgeous country."

"I'm jealous you live here," I said.

Rocky entered the room with a full plate of food.

"Hungry?" she said. "Who's up for lunch?"

She sat next to Colin and smiled at him. Their love for one another could be seen in an instant. Then she looked up.

"Did you see the giraffe again?" Rocky asked Colin. "I saw one running near the house!" They were never unfazed by the sight of an animal.

As I wanted to stress, the Francombe family was as generous and uniquely wonderful as any other family you might encounter. When you met them you were eagerly introduced under the assumption that you had always been their family; it had just been a long time since you decided to track them down. In their home, we felt like guests who have always had a bed tucked in awaiting our arrival. Tourism didn't reach inside of their fences. Tourism was far from this place.

Our days at Ol Malo, although long and full, passed quickly. It only took a few mornings to acclimate to the new customs, the new routine, or—since routine was only attempted—a new way of life, as many called it. I began to look forward to the quiet knock on my door announcing that even though the sun was still sleeping, a fresh cup of Kenyan coffee sat steaming at my doorstep. Equally, I embraced the ability to take a cup outside to watch the light begin to shine over the vast country as I quietly listened to the dawn of a different world. I welcomed the early mornings (which is admittedly unlike me) and the long days that they symbolized. The meals were far from overlooked. A breakfast of bacon, toast, eggs, fruit, and cereal was always served to start our day properly. These were naturally followed by a morning drive with Colin out into the wild. The days were perfectly planned so that we'd return for lunch at Ol Malo, have some down time to relax in the gorgeous setting, and then trek out again to simply see what we could find. Of course, four o'clock English tea was never missed. Our hectic minds slowly began to unwind as we embraced the new lifestyle.

One thing I will mention, that I was unaware of before my visit, is the fact that you wouldn't see all of the African species in every location. It was a naive presumption, I realize, but for some reason I just thought you'd see lions and tigers and bears everywhere you went (well, at least lions). But every terrain is fit for certain types of life and not others, and Africa is no different. Ol Malo was abundant with giraffe and zebra, although elephant were sparse in the area. We were not able to spot elephant on the trip until we departed Ol Malo and flew to Lewa Downs a few days later.

Admiring the animal kingdom was only a minor part of what intrigued me about the country. While it was quite surreal seeing the entire region's food chain in a matter of hours, the people and their culture were far more fascinating. Africa brought us closer to the European descendants of adventurous British aristocrats, like the Francombes. The visit also introduced us to the native Africans who now both share and fight for the land they live on. That's not to imply that the British of Kenya aren't fighting just as hard to protect the community. Their determination to maintain and even improve the sacred life they encountered shall not be overlooked. Yet the indigenous people literally still prepare, depart, and return from war just as every generation before them has. They do this in the same manner and with the same weapons as always.

The Francombes were friends of the *Samburu*. They shared the same land. In Africa you only do that with those you trust. I don't mean that they lived right next door. The Samburu community was miles away from Ol Malo. But in Africa, the fact that they lived only miles away meant that they shared the same land. They were good friends. They looked out for one another. They had to.

The Samburu invited our family to watch them perform a very special ritual. They were planning a war dance, literally. Word had spread to the tribe that our family was staying with the Francombes. The Samburu extended us an invitation. We, of course, went.

To see them perform the ritual, not for show, but for us as guests, was a great honor. It's not very often that you get to spy on foreign ritual that is done in pure spirit and not for the sake of an audience or education. True, we were obvious visitors, yet if we hadn't been there, the ceremony would still have taken place.

I stood in awe as the red-haired warriors gathered together, with their spears held tightly in hand. The Samburu, a sort of mountain-ous version of the Masai you've probably heard about, were elaborately covered in their traditional red and white garments, jewelry, and paint.

Walking through the gate and into the barren village was like opening a vault that held an entirely new perspective. Never before had I been faced with a culture as different from my own. There was not a single sign of the modern life I knew anywhere—not a similarity in sight. Facial expressions were our only form of communication. The Samburu warriors gave us much-appreciated nods and smiles. Then they gathered close together into an ancient huddle. They began jumping in unison, with our family and the local women surrounding them on the perimeter. The synchronistic jumping then stopped. The dance began to single out the warriors. Each took his turn jumping on his own, jumping for us, jumping for the Samburu, jumping in celebration of the life he knew. The pride in their eyes could not be mistaken.

These Samburu warriors had recently returned from war—war over land, war with the same tribes they've fought for centuries. Unusual was the lone warrior who stood out from the crowd with his long, braided hair. We later learned that the Samburu warriors shave their heads when a family member dies in battle. All but one of the twenty or so young men had hair no longer than half an inch, a sign of the war's recent and large presence.

We vaguely understood their lives and they vaguely understood ours. As far as I could tell, we weren't even foreigners, but rather Martians, true Martians coming down from the sky to visit their isolated community. You could see it most in the children. As our Land Rover drove into the village on our arrival, the children all ran to the edge of the road just to catch a curious glimpse. We waved. They stared back in awe, waving, giggling ... staring. The older Samburu had encountered more of our kind, or at least were old enough not to look shocked by our arrival. Yet the whites of their eyes still dug into the whites of ours, as we both took turns facing a culture that intrigued us beyond belief or comprehension.

It's not your average day when you meet with a tribe of Samburu warriors. It was quite the out-of-body type of experience. Yet those are not the moments I remember most. As with all occasions spent with extraordinary people, our times at Ol Malo were made special by Rocky and Colin.

"Wasn't that incredible?" Rocky asked us once we had walked back to their home. "I still get chills watching that dance."

"Do you know them by name?" asked Taylor.

"Who, the Samburu?" said Rocky, as she was putting flowers into a vase. "Yes, most of them. Our daughter, Julia, works with them. We're like old friends now."

"What does Julia do?" I asked.

"She started a foundation," said Rocky. "She works with the children to sell their art in America. The profits go a long way over here."

My everlasting memories of our visit are of Rocky and Colin, not the things they showed us. You can't complain when you pile into a jeep and head out into desolation, only to find each corner's new view more breathtaking than the last. But while I am one of the world's biggest fans of places, it is the things that happen there and people you encounter that make them alluring. If you're only interested in seeing lions, I suggest you order a *National Geographic* video and stay at home.

7

The Masai Mara

"Paul! The mountain!" my mom yelled, as she gripped the edge of her seat.

"I see it!" I yelled back stubbornly. I *was* aimed a little low.

The controls felt awkward, different than I had imagined. It was not like driving a car. In fact, I can't say I got used to them at all. I flew the plane for a good ten minutes before handing control back to the pilot. I still never hit the comfort zone. It felt looser than it should, wobblier. Yet all new sailors zigzag on their first try; it's your natural instinct. I could see how once you felt the winds fill the sail a few times the plane would make sense and feel true behind your hands. I never reached that point.

"So, here I am flying a plane," I thought, "in Kenya. Not a bad day." With that notion I even turned around to ensure my family felt the same way. Only, I saw terror in their eyes as my focus left the road. I smiled, of course. It was a great day to be flying. I didn't enjoy departing from the Francombes. I wasn't ready to leave. You're never ready to leave. But as we said our good-byes, Rocky and Colin's brightened expressions persuaded me that much was awaiting our arrival. For now there was no anxiety about arriving. I was excited about the getting there.

There's a big difference between dozing off in a jet thirty thousand feet above the ground and zipping across the plains low enough to spot wildlife—a good difference. In a jet you feel slightly sheltered, as you pass through the clouds and look out over the vast haze covering the earth. In a bush plane you feel alive. The engine roars loudly as you putter through the air. The thin doors of the plane shut, but rattle. Conversation isn't possible. Words are sucked directly into the propellers. You are forced to listen only to your eyes, as they sweep across the landscape. When you look down, the view appears less like a picture on television and more like the opening scene of an IMAX film. The earth moves beneath the plane like the ocean rushing past your feet in the wake of a sandy shore. One second you are gliding, the next your stomach is sitting in a roller coaster. Turbulence in a bush plane feels more like a ship riding out the pummeling waves of a deep Atlantic storm and less like a minor speed bump in a smoothly paved neighborhood. Safe and secure are the last feelings to surround you. You lose the relaxing daydreams. You are forced into exhilarating reality. The wind is right next to you, not outside. For once you actually feel like you are flying. What a day to sit behind the wheel!

We landed that afternoon in the great plains of Kenya, in the Masai Mara. Something about the Mara set it apart from the other locations. Somehow I felt that we had truly arrived at the heart of Africa. We killed the engine and let the propellers spin through the open air. This was the place where I discovered what the term *open air* meant. Everything is simply bigger in Kenya. Everything was simply biggest in the Mara. The plains were wider, much wider than in Kansas. Not a single hill was in sight. And with the larger locale came different animals, and more of them. I mentioned earlier that you could not see every African species in a single location. That was a blanket statement. All blanket statements have exceptions. The Masai Mara was the exception. You could see *everything* there. I believe we did. We slept in tents, not in villas. We ate most meals in the field, not at base camp. The Masai Mara just felt like Africa should feel.

Speaking of those *National Geographic* clips I mentioned earlier, which we all like more than we'll admit—you know the clips. They're the ones where the lion is lying stealthily low in the tall grass, spying on the casual zebras grazing in the plain. Suddenly the lion springs to his feet and chases the zebras across the field. The camera zooms out to show you how much ground they're covering. You have a split second to notice those weird-looking trees in the background. Outside of those trees, there is nothing else nearby for miles. But then you see that *one* thing is nearby; the camera zooms in and you notice the lion is near the zebras now—real near. The lion gets closer. Then closer. Then he strikes. Those are the clips I'm talking about. They were filmed in the Mara, or the Serengeti, but they're the same field. Literally. The Masai Mara and the Serengeti *are* the same field; they only have a different name depending on which country you are in. But the Serengeti tends to steal most of the credit, for some reason. Maybe the name *Serengeti* is more appealing or more romantic. The name sounds like a place in Italy. Who knows? But just so you know: if you're in Tanzania, you're in the Serengeti. If you're in Kenya, you're in the Mara. You shouldn't care which one you're in, as long as you're in one of them. The land is amazing.

Our guide, Jackson Loosoiya, grew up in these plains. His father, a recidivist poacher-turned-game department ranger, once took Jackson on a four-month hunting trip when Jackson was a young boy. Jackson, fluent in English, was now showing us the same places and animals that his father had revealed to him. Jackson was a natural teacher as well.

His unusually tall and full build for a Masai matched his aspirations. As documented in *Travel and Leisure's* 2001 issue on Africa's best safari guides, "The future of the country is people like Jackson."

Jackson was well versed in much more than Kenyan culture, although he didn't pretend to be above it. Jackson was a local Kenyan, proud and true. Yet he was constantly surrounded by the thoughts and ideas of people from around the world. Jackson used that experience to advance himself immensely. It also didn't hurt that he was friendly as hell.

"It's great to have you here," said Jackson upon our arrival. "I love people from Atlanta—always friendly. Did the Carters have a good time?"

"Of course," said my dad. "They always have a good time! Spoke the world of you."

"I'm just glad they enjoyed themselves," said Jackson, humbled.

"How long have you lived here?" asked Taylor.

"Forever," said Jackson, "although I get away more than you'd think. I was in Atlanta about a year ago. I spent some time with Phil Osbourne, marketing the company. Atlanta's a great spot. Not like here, though; I miss it when I have to leave."

Rekero, the camp we stayed at, was developed by a member of the Beaton family. The Beatons rank in the "famous" category when speaking of British Kenyans. Captain Duncan Beaton arrived in Africa in 1889 from the Isle of Skye, on the west coast of Scotland. (By the way, how'd we let our society get to the point where we can't show up at Le Cirque with a reservation under the name "Captain"?) Captain Beaton was an agent for the African Lakes Corporation. The company was formed to carry on the work of David Livingstone in the suppression of the slave trade and the opening up of commerce of Central Africa.

Captain Beaton's son, Ken Beaton, was born on a Portuguese gunboat in the mouth of the Zambesi River, at a village called Chinde, in what is present-day Mozambique. No shit. He was. I just thought that was worth sharing.

I heard the zipper on my tent being quickly ripped toward the ground.

"Paul, wake up." It was Jackson. "Do you hear them?"

"Yeah," I responded. "Are they close?"

"Yeah. Real close. Probably two hundred yards."

The deep rumble of the lion's call had woken me only a few minutes ago. The grunt seemed to fill our tent like faint rolling thunder, nearing with each rustle. If Jackson had told me the lion was ten yards away I would have believed him.

We had spotted our first pack of lions earlier in the night on the way back to camp from a drive. But that was miles away. Not next to our tent! Yes, armed guards watched over our compound throughout the night. But how much do you trust a guard against an animal that stays alive by stalking unwary prey? Knowing the guards are there brings comfort, but not a nice warm and fuzzy feeling. It's not that lion attacks are common in the first place—but as far as I'm concerned, the lion will remain at the top of the food chain if it wants to.

Instead of Jackson telling Taylor and me not to worry and that the lion wouldn't bother us if we didn't bother him, Jackson looked at me with a large grin, and asked, "Do you want to go find him?"

Taylor didn't find the idea of purposefully stalking lions in the middle of the night to be at the top of her list of things she personally craved to do. My mom seemed to feel the same way. I think Dad would have gone. Yet he didn't find the idea of leaving his two girls alone in the tents while he stalked lions in the middle of the night to be at the top of things he should do either. Not if he wanted to stay married. So it was down to me and Jackson.

We quickly jumped into the Land Rover and began to drive out of the camp. Jackson stopped at the edge of the compound and picked up an older Masai man, who I learned upon introduction spoke no English. "He'll be helpful," Jackson responded to my unvoiced question. "With him as our eyes, we'll find him for sure." I didn't see how much good our eyes would do in the pitch-black dark, but then Jackson turned on a searchlight and handed it to our tracker. The two spoke for a moment in Masai dialect. Then the tracker pointed out into the dark. We turned the vehicle and moved out.

We began a pattern of driving to a new spot, scanning the perimeter with the light, turning off the light to listen in silence, and moving on to a more likely location. After countless repetitions of our pattern I began to lose hope. The lion's call, which I have to disclose is far from the famous growl seen at the beginning of movies, could be heard in the distance. We never seemed to close in on it. Then, after a disappointing lack of sound for quite some time, the lion stepped out of the dark. Far down the beaten path we seemed to be following, the male entered our beam. He began to walk in our direction. I assumed we would only catch a glimpse as he crossed the path and headed out into the tall, protective grass. He had other intentions.

Like a lazy human, he chose the easier route. The lion began walking down the old jeep road toward us. As he neared, I sat in wonder. I contemplated the beauty in his mane, coat, and confident gait. Not scared off by either the searchlight or our presence, the lion continued walking directly toward us. As I was thinking that he must turn away eventually, he slowly moved along and strolled within only a few feet of our vehicle. Rolling his eyes in our direction, seemingly staring deep into the eyes of each one of us, he silently communicated his authority before walking casually down the path and out of sight.

I was shocked at how little we bothered him. He was the conqueror of the area. It was almost frightening the way he disregarded our intrusion on his territory. The way he looked at us only confirmed my thought that this was his domain. He was going to do just as he pleased. The lion had an unusual manner about him, unlike any other animal I'd ever seen. There was literally not a single ounce of fear in his body. If you look hard enough at any person, or at any animal, you'll usually catch a glimpse of fear somewhere—not here. Not with this lion. He managed to easily convey that our technological superiority was no match for his natural power and grace. Somehow his pride was quite nice to see, similar to that of the Masai.

The following morning we sat down to another lengthy breakfast. I couldn't stop talking about the lion. I must have told the same story three times at least. Everyone seemed relieved when I had to stop my story as we all looked up at an unexpected vehicle headed toward camp. Gerard Beaton, in a worn Land Rover, slowly drove up and parked next to our table.

Gerard brought company. Company in Kenya is guaranteed to be interesting simply for the fact that they as well are in Kenya; this weeds out a large portion of the boring types. Guess who he brings? Georgians, of course! Not people from the country of Georgia. These were not close relatives of anyone from Russia. No one stumbled out of the Land Rover with crisp vodka clinging to their breath and speaking a harsh language we didn't comprehend. I'm talking about Georgians! Neighbors! Southern folk with a slight twang in their voices. I'm beginning to think they just send everyone from Georgia to the same places in the same week to spare everyone our company. Maybe they do that in all places? Were all the people from Chicago in the other half of the country?

These were special Georgians. They were special because they were daring. These were about to be the first foreign tourists to enter Uganda since the last ones who went didn't return. Why go there? To see gorillas. Why not go there? To see guerillas. The group that didn't return saw the wrong kind. Yeah. Not good. Not the goal. The other kind is better. Way better.

Uganda had been under political strife for quite some time. Too much strife for some people. So much strife that tourists began to get murdered. Rebel armies have long existed in various parts of East and Central Africa: the Lord's Resistance Army operates to the north of Bwindi, and the Interahamwe—the extremist Hum group responsible for the slaughter of more than eight hundred thousand people in Rwanda and Burundi in 1994—has a faction to the west. The Interahamwe blame America, Britain, and Uganda for backing minority Tutsi rule in Rwanda after the genocide. As an act of protest and publicity, the Interahamwe had recently kidnapped and murdered a group of gorilla tourists on safari. The killings ended gorilla tourism in Uganda for quite some time—for obvious reasons.

We ate breakfast with the couple that still wanted to see gorillas.

"We think the situation is under control and that it is plenty safe now," they said.

"Do you really think so?" asked my mother, worried for their safety.

"We do; shouldn't be dangerous anymore."

"I'm not sure you could get me in there!" laughed my dad.

"Somebody's got to be the first to go back in." They were definitely a brave couple. Luckily, they are safe and sound. I'm sure it was a fabulous trip too (although maybe accompanied by a *little* uneasiness, as well as a *little* annoyance at the news crew). They were nice people to have breakfast with. It's not often that we eat breakfast with new people.

That afternoon, Taylor and I lounged around the camp, killing time before the next drive. As we sat playing backgammon, still full from a hearty lunch, Taylor looked anxious. She was not wearing her usual smile.

"Double threes," I said. I picked up my checkers and moved them toward the rack, creating a new point along the way.

"You're going to win," she said. "I think that did it."

"I don't know," I replied. "You've still got a shot."

"What time's the next drive?" she asked, as she looked at her watch.

"Think we're got about an hour," I said.

"I'm tired of waiting around all day," she said. "I'm ready to get back home, I think."

"Really?" I asked. "I'd stay for weeks."

"I know you would," she said.

"What are you in such a hurry for?" I asked.

"I miss seeing everyone," she said.

"We've only been gone a few weeks," I responded.

"That's a long time," she replied. "Besides, we've been doing the same thing every day since we got here."

"Every day's been different," I said.

"No," she replied. "Every day has been the same. We wake up, eat breakfast, go on a drive, eat lunch, lounge around, go on another drive, eat dinner, and go to bed."

"I think it's great," I said. "Besides, you're making it sound worse than it is."

"I've had fun," she said. "I'm just ready to get back to see everyone."

"They aren't going anywhere," I replied.

"I know," she said. "But we aren't either."

Taylor is three years younger than me. At the time, she was in early high school and completely caught up in home. She felt that if she left the scene for even a few weeks, people would forget she existed and write her off as old news. I knew where she was coming from. I tried to teach her that her friends weren't going anywhere, if they were her friends, and that upon our return things would be exactly as we had left them. I tried to help her enjoy the moment, but she is a stubborn bird. Taylor had made up her mind. She was ready to leave. What frustrated me most was not that she wanted to leave, but the painful truth that she was going to get her wish soon. Our trip was nearing an end.

After the game of backgammon, I wandered over to see what my parents were doing with the downtime. As expected, my father was taking a nap. My mother was sitting comfortably in her chair, reading.

"How's the book?" I asked her.

"Can't put it down," she said. "What've ya'll been up to?"

"Backgammon," I said. "Tay and I just finished a game."

"Is she still anxious to get home?" she asked.

"Yeah," I said. "I think she's seen one too many zebras."

"I wish she would cheer up," she said. "I hate seeing her in a bad mood."

"It's not like her," I replied. "I miss having her laughing all day, like usual."

"She misses her friends, I think," Mom said.

"Yeah, that's what she implied. You ready to get home to the gallery?"

"It's been nice to get away," she said, "but should be fun once we get back. We've got some big shows coming up."

"Anyone I know?"

"Mario Petrirena is having another show soon," she said.

"I love his stuff," I replied.

"I know. I just bought another piece of his to put in the living room."

"Well, I guess I'll go delve into my book as well," I said.

"Okay, see you in a bit," she replied. "It's nice out, should be a good drive later."

There could not have been a better place to have a drink than the spot we chose on our last night in Africa. Actually, we chose two locations to have sunsetters, partially because it was our last night, partially because there were two places we needed to see, and mainly because we were in Kenya and had nothing else to do but drive around to scenic spots drinking sunsetters.

Sunsetters are a good idea. They're a great idea, actually. First of all, if you're having a sunsetter you're in a good mood. You're in a good mood because you are in a gorgeous place. You are taking time out of your day to ensure that you are doing nothing more than as little as possible. Your only focus is on which type of sunsetter would match the hour best. You're in that window of time when the sun is struggling to shed its favorite light for as long as possible. The early evening is by far my favorite time of the day.

We stood on a large—extremely large—boulder (large enough to require about a five-minute hike to its peak) that put us in a prime location. Far beneath our toes, below and as far as we could see into the distance, there was nothing but vast open prairie expanding out into the purple light until Kilimanjaro climbed out of nowhere, jutting boldly into the sky. What amazed me was not the breathtaking panorama. It was not that sensation of overwhelming accomplishment I felt the last time I stood atop a large boulder. It was not the feeling of false sadness that hits you when you realize how much you've done in such little time and that that time is now over. It was not even how great the Kenyan beer tasted, even though it could have been a little colder, as *all* Kenyan beers could be.

No, what amazed me was the fact that out in the distance, somewhere within our breathtaking view—as my family stood together, laughing, smiling, taking in one last glimpse of this foreign sun, gazing out at the lone mountain towering in the sky, thousands of miles from home, looking out past the horizon into the places and people that comprised our recent memories—Chas and his father stood on a mountain, nearing the peak, cherishing their time together as we did the same, looking out at a new world, laughing, smiling, taking in one last glimpse of the day's foreign sun. They stood on Kilimanjaro. They were right across the plain.

Paul Hudson and Chas Smithgall at a roadside stop in Kansas

Justin Rainer, Paul Hudson, and Donald Houser

Donald, Paul, and Justin at the Ilium campgrounds in Telluride

Justin, Donald, and Chas relaxing at camp

Paul and Donald in western Colorado

Justin and Donald on the drive to Moab

Justin on the Slickrock Trail in Moab, Utah

Paul admiring the view in Moab

Colin Francombe, Paul, and Debbie Hudson at Ol Malo, Kenya

Taylor, Debbie, and Paul on an afternoon safari

Paul and Debbie Hudson in front of Mount Kilimanjaro

Jackson, a local guide, and Paul in the Masai Mara.

Debbie and Paul Hudson in the Masai Mara

Taylor and Paul

Taylor posing for a picture on an afternoon drive

Taylor in a Masai village

Sunset in the Masai Mara

PART II

Montana

8

Circular Reasoning

My first year in Charlottesville vanished. In what felt like weeks, a year had gone by without anyone telling me. Next thing I knew, it was May. Damn! But adventure was lingering. Chas, Donald, Justin, and I were off to work on a cattle ranch in Montana. His aunt and uncle, Sherry and Eddie, had invited us out for the summer. That was not an invitation you would turn down.

Not much happens in Montana. That's the beauty of it all. Granted, some things do happen, but not the kind of things you're used to. Not the kind of things that itch your comfort. Different things.

Not much happens on a ranch, especially. Well, things happen, but you don't really notice them. That's the goal. No one tries to *change* a ranch. All you try to do is keep it the same. A ranch is in its perfect state from the beginning. That's what attracts us to ranches. I guess it is true that a ranch is initially burdened by the fences we build around it. The ranch would prefer that the fences were never built. But as the rains pour down on the fences and slowly weather their rusted souls, the fences eventually become part of the place. At that point, even the ranch itself starts to love its own fences, like a father looking after his son. So, you have to keep up the fences. You have to keep up the land. You have to keep up the animals. It sounds easy, but it is damn hard work.

A ranch hand fails if deterioration shows. He also fails if everything suddenly appears brand new. That's not the way a ranch is supposed to look. It can't look any better than it did before you arrived, in its purity, so you try to keep it that way.

Cattle and escape—those were the two reasons this ranch existed. Escape was the real reason, but cattle determined the daily pattern. Cattle determined the seasonal pattern as well. I'll start with the seasonal one and then break it down from there.

It's pretty simple. You grow hay for the cattle when there's not snow on the ground. You feed the cattle with the hay when there's snow on the ground. Of course it's not *that* simple, but that's the gist of the basic structure. There are deeper layers within the structure, which I'll get to. I just wanted you to grasp the larger picture first. We weren't waiters on a dude ranch. We were ranch hands on a cattle ranch. Now, I don't want to lead you astray. We weren't cowboys. We wanted to be, but we weren't. Who doesn't want to be a cowboy? We didn't grow up on the land, know the land, become the land. We were literally extra hands who helped out where we could. And of course, we were pampered. I'm not trying to pretend that we weren't. We had a free place to stay, free transportation, free gas, and more free food than we could have asked for. I mean, these are the Wachses we're talking about. It was hard work, but it was some of the most gratifying work that I've ever done.

Ranch work isn't enjoyable by nature. The work isn't like the law or philosophy; no one does it simply because of what it stands for. In fact, the physical exertion that is ranch work can be quite awful. And sometimes your body isn't even being physically exerted. Sometimes the exertion is just in your mind. There's a large amount of monotony in many of the tasks. The monotony can drip down on your face like a drop of water until it becomes physically painful. But you begin to love the work. You begin to respect the work for its purity. Eventually, you attach yourself to it. You become a part of the fence. These were good fences to be a part of.

Circles. Large circles. Most of my time on the ranch was spent in large circles. Circles started large, then dwindled themselves down until they were indecipherable. Countless fields were scattered across the ranch, waiting in anticipation of our circular treatment. We gave them more of a haircut than a massage, but you've got to think the fields enjoyed it, nonetheless. Why the circles? I'll dig down a layer into the pattern to explain.

Grow hay for the cattle when there's not snow on the ground. Feed the cattle with the hay when there's snow on the ground. We arrived on July 4, 2000, during the height of the hay-growing season. Within the broad pattern of the seasons, there are smaller patterns, many of them, organized like a series of smaller circles drawn within the original. Growing hay when there's not snow on the ground entails a simple repetitive process. Over a month or so, barren fields will eventually produce a large amount of hay. You cut down the hay, store it, then let the barren fields grow again. In a good season you will get multiple cuts from the fields. We were there for only one cut. Our entire time on the ranch involved only a notch in the pattern.

As you may have picked up, we were not crucial to the process. We were not hired out of dire necessity. Things worked before our arrival. Things worked after our departure. Eddie and Sherry Wachs hired us for other reasons. First, ranch work is good for you. It is tiring, physical, grueling, hot, and thus makes you a stronger person in many ways. Second, the Wachses are some of the most generous people that I have ever met. They wanted to share their ranch with us. They wanted us to enjoy it as if it were our own. Third, in many ways, we were their children. Parents like spending time with their children.

Eddie and Sherry only had two children, and they were Labrador retrievers. Trust me when I tell you: they were their children. You know how many people have dogs that they enjoy, and like to have around the house? You know how, within that group of people, there are those who have dogs that they love deeply and have strong attachments to? You know how within that group of people there are the select few who have dogs that they love so much that they treat them as equals within in the family, because they literally *are* in the family? The Wachses are that kind of people. Out of a giant sweep of luck, we were considered their children too. They invited us to the ranch so they could keep us at home for a summer and simply watch us grow up.

I still haven't explained the circles. As you are hopefully beginning to feel, a ranch is one big series of patterns within other patterns. Within each pattern lie a thousand more, each one more intricate than its parent. Eventually, as this series of patterns must, it gets to be so detailed, so minute that you can't distinguish the pattern except to know that it is there. This is the reason people live on ranches. They live for the things they can't describe. They can live forever on the millimeters because they know that they add up to meters, and even kilometers, over time. The same goes for Kenya. The same goes for Colorado. The same goes for the road. But you can't live forever on the road. That's why there are places like Montana. The key thing to remember is that every place has its own intricacies and patterns. You've just got to figure out which patterns match your sense of color, that's all.

So, why the circles? With each cut, you start your blade at the edge of the field and wind yourself along that edge until the edge is gone. You do this in circles. I guess you could do it horizontally. For some reason, that just doesn't feel right. Straight lines don't go along with the pattern. Straight lines end. They don't wind themselves down. They just don't make any sense on a ranch.

The comforting thing is that the pattern continues. Cutting the field is only one layer. You then have to gather the hay. That's not as easy as it sounds. This calls for many more patterns. You can't just walk out into a field and bag the hay, like leaves in autumn. You have to bale the hay. But you can't just bale the hay once it is cut; the process is not that simple. The hay is too spread out. It wouldn't bale right. Besides, that wouldn't be enough patterns. So, you rake the hay closer together. Not by hand, by tractor. In circles.

A massive rake, about twenty yards wide, is attached to the back of the trailer. The rake is perfectly sized so that, as it rolls behind you, the outer edges of the rake just barely stretch to cover two cuts of the blade. The rake is slanted inward, so that as you move throughout the field it gathers the two thin cuts on its outer edges and funnels them together into a single row. As the pattern goes, you wind yourself around the field, each distance being closer to the middle than the last, until, once again, you reach the intricate center. Now you can bale the hay.

Yet you don't wait that long to bale. That wouldn't be efficient. You could if you had fewer hands, but we had the hands, so we used them. The baler, in a separate tractor, would begin only moments after the raker. In a sense, the raker is the wave and the baler is the surfer, in a much slower fashion, of course.

The baler would drive on top of your wake for a few hundred yards, to collect the hay, until the bin was full. He would then pause, pray that it wasn't jammed, then allow the square machine to process the hay into the bale. Of course, the bale, as you've all seen, is of a particularly fitting shape. A circle. At the end of all the circles, of all the patterns, lie condensed circles representing all of the patterns in one. And, of course, this isn't the end. You later have to collect all of the bales and store them together, so that you can use them for food in the winter. And to make a long story short, the cows eat the hay, the cows process the hay, you use the results as fertilizer, and the next season you can begin cutting the fields again. These are only a few of the patterns that take place on a ranch.

Although we all took turns at the wheel, I tended to rake when we were in the field. In fact, I never baled. But the rest baled. And the rest also raked. The rest were Donald, Justin, and Chas, of course. Some of the best moments on the ranch took place when the raker passed the baler in the field. Sometimes you would look over and wave. Sometimes you would just nod. Other times you would simply stare ahead into the calm ocean in front of you. But there was always an acknowledgment of the other's presence with each pass. And it was more than just an acknowledgment of presence. The acknowledgment was a joyful comprehension that each of us was living out the pattern—not reading about the pattern, or watching the pattern, or hearing about the pattern, but *living* the pattern. There's much to be said for that. And to celebrate, we played music. And we played it loud. You see, when you work on a ranch of this size, you have *large* tractors, enclosed tractors with radios. What station did we play? Do I even have to say it? Are you going to make me? It wasn't rock and roll. It was far from rap. It had a little twang to it. And raspy sounding guitars. What else would you want to listen to on a tractor?

Eighteen thousand acres—that was a lot of ranch to look after. In fact, it was *two* ranches, or at least, one ranch with two names. You've got to love ranches so large that they have two names. You might have thought the place was two ranches, if you drove down the old dirt road past Trails End Ranch and found yourself at the gates of Hollow Top Ranch a few miles away. But the land was the same. The same, in that they were both ours. The same, in that they were both the Wachses'. And, if you know land, you know that if you can cross different sections of the land and still feel like you're at home, then the place is one and the same. You could do that here.

There *were* multiple houses though. The names, in all practical conversation and meaning, really only referred to the houses. At Trails End, a one-story log cabin sat nestled in the early part of a developing plain left by a mountain's disappearing edge. The cabin had a quiet, meandering stream for a neighbor, a small stream no wider than a stretch of the legs. The stream passed by the edge of a wooden fence that enclosed the comfortable green yard in which the cabin sat. Of course there was a porch, with rocking chairs. And the chairs rocked in the direction of a barn, a beautiful massive barn with wide, tall doors. The Wachses slept at Trails End. We slept at Hollow Top.

Hollow Top was the name of the mountain that hovered over the town of Pony. What a name for a Montana town—Pony, Montana. That sounded good enough to me. A bar and a post office, that's Pony. Of course, the town used to have more. As with all old mining towns, life once existed on a much larger scale. This town, which lies on the eastern slope of the Tobacco Root Mountains, in the south-west part of the state, used to have jewelers, druggists, hotels, restaurants, brothels—the usual mining necessities.

N. J. Isdell, a native New Yorker, opened the general store in 1892. Yet, as far as I could tell, only the Pony Bar and the post office were still open for business. You had to drive to Harrison for gas. And lunch. And really, for everything but beer and stamps. Not that Harrison had much commerce. You had to drive thirty miles to Ennis to rent a decent movie. But you don't need much in Montana. Harrison made do much more than I would have expected. In fact, so did Pony. What more do you need, besides food and beer, after working on a ranch all day? Right at our cabin we had a full standing freezer with all the steaks and hamburgers you would ever need. We *were* living on a cattle ranch. And just up the road was the Pony Bar. What a classic place.

Pony was once a booming town. That is, if having a population of a thousand residents classified a town as "booming." But you didn't classify a mining town for its people, not in the 1800s. Booming meant gold. Five million dollars' worth. Five million dollars is a lot for the 1800s. Two Virginia City businessmen, W. W. Morris and Henry Elling, were the lucky keepers of most of that money. Over a few years, they bought up almost all the gold mines in the entire area. The mines had Western names, such as the Boss Tweed, the Clipper, Willow Creek, and the Strawberry.

Of course, I knew none of this history the night we arrived at the ranch, July 4, 2000. Regrettably, all of the stories I am sharing about the places in this book up to this point, I did not know during the time I was there. It wasn't until April 3, 2002, the date I decided to write this book, that I began blowing off the dust.

What happened that morning that caused me to begin writing this? I woke up extremely frustrated, which is unlike me. I was so worried about getting the proper job (to no avail) that it was eating away at my self-esteem. It was eating away at my enjoyment of just about everything that I used to love. So, that got me thinking. *What do I love?* It sure wasn't the jobs I found myself interviewing for. It sure wasn't being a wreck all day and stressing about everything. What I loved were my experiences that led me to be stress free. What I loved was traveling the world with my friends and discovering everything that's out there. And the jobs I was looking at seemed to hold the key to a future jail cell. I woke up in rebellion and decided to share my story, in fear that these experiences were going to be locked away from me forever. I wanted to inspire everyone I could—especially those younger than me, with their entire lives ahead of them—to get out there on their own, to travel the world, and fall in love with its wonders. Hopefully, you are enjoying the aftermath.

9
Trails End Ranch

The day we first drove down the long, dusty road to Trails End Ranch was one of my better ones. We woke from a few hours of much-needed sleep in a hotel in the town of Billings. After a quick stop for chicken biscuits—which was fatally unsuccessful, since the local Montanans had a dreadful time understanding that chicken biscuits to most folks means that you get a biscuit with chicken *in* it, not just the biscuits that go *along* with chicken—we were able to move on, although we were starving. The Yellowstone River was our guide for most of the morning, as we headed up the highway, following its path.

It took us two days to get to Billings. Not bad—Atlanta, Georgia, to Billings, Montana, in two days. The beautiful thing is that we were experienced at it. If you recall, the last summer we had driven to St. Louis and thought that was a major feat for a first day's drive. Not anymore. We passed the St. Louis arch on a midafternoon stroll. We only ate dinner in Kansas City and still put some miles on the odometer. We were, as you could have guessed, in the mood for something quite good to eat after driving from Atlanta to Kansas City by dinnertime. So, what did we do? We didn't get off the highway and drive around aimlessly, which had previously proved to be useless.

I made a phone call. "Kansas City, Missouri … the Ritz-Carlton."

"Hudson, what are you doing? Is that 4-1-1?" asked Donald.

"Yes, is this the Ritz?" I said, once I was connected. "Where are you located?"

We drove right into the nice part of the city. There were too many steak houses in the area to choose from. We settled for the Kansas City Grill, as it sounded appropriate.

"Feels good to be on the road again," Justin remarked at dinner.

"Ya'll are going to love Montana," Chas added. "We're talking big country."

"Makes Colorado feel small, I hear," added Donald.

"Mountains aren't as tall, but it is wide open," said Chas.

"How long have Eddie and Sherry owned the ranch?" asked Justin.

"As long as I can remember," said Chas.

"Can you remember anything after that four-wheeler crash?" Donald said jokingly, trying to push Chas's buttons.

"I remember that I can still kick your ass when needed," Chas said with a laugh.

When Chas was younger he had been in an ATV accident on the ranch in Montana. In all seriousness, it was a pretty bad accident, and he's lucky he's all right. Chas has a small scar on his forehead as a reminder.

"Look forward to seeing Eddie and Sherry again," I said.

"I know," we all seemed to say in unison. "I know."

After dinner, we were eager to pay the bill so we could continue pushing along. We rested that night in Omaha, Nebraska. The next day was almost entirely South Dakota and Wyoming. The most exciting part of that day (or so this particular road makes you feel) was, sadly, getting to Wall Drug. Wall Drug is not a drugstore. Wall Drug is one of those tourist attractions that makes up the entire town, the town of Wall, South Dakota. Why Wall Drug? Simply because there is nothing else to do in South Dakota but trap tourists. And, I mean, we were *excited* to get there. Real excited. You have to be excited. There's a damn sign for it every single mile on the road. Literally. For hundreds of miles. Big signs, too. "Wall Drug—5 cent Coffee." "Wall Drug—We're Going to Advertise So Freaking Much That You *Have* to Stop Here." I mean, man! We heard a rumor, and I buy into it completely, that the first sign for Wall Drug is in the good ol' state of

Maine! And of course, Wall Drug is awful. Don't go there. Don't give them any credit. It wasn't the best part of our day because we loved it. It was the best part of our day because we were *past* it. No more signs. That was the highlight.

Passing Wall Drug was even more exciting than seeing Mount Rushmore and the Badlands. It was Fourth of July weekend, and for some reason every hillbilly on the road seemed to be swarming to the place. And that meant traffic. We drove close enough to barely make out the presidents' faces, and I mean *barely*, before turning around and getting the hell out of there. And, just so you know, Mount Rushmore is not just off the highway, like they make it seem. It is miles and miles away. As far as our experience went, it was not worth a three-minute detour. (Sorry, Abe.)

Passing Wall beat the Badlands as well. Why? When we reached the park we paid fifteen bucks for a helicopter tour. We didn't realize that for fifteen bucks they fly you to the edge of the park and go, "There are the Badlands," and then fly you back to the gravel parking lot. You'd be amazed at the gimmicks they come up with on the road. At first, you buy into them all. That's part of the fun. But after a while you can drive by, content knowing that some sucker is losing his money while you're getting that much closer to a nice meal and some rest.

I digressed. The day we first drove down the long, dusty road to Trails End Ranch was one of my better ones. Each ranch we saw could've been ours, especially when we knew we were close. Each fence, each house, each pasture—we had no idea. I thought about ten ranches were the one we were going to live on. Each one was perfect while I was thinking that, including Trails End.

Let me lay out our first hour there. Keep in mind, we were nineteen-year-old boys at this point in time. Keep in mind even more that we were boys in general.

We drove down the long, dusty road to Trails End Ranch and arrived at a perfect rustic setting. Within five minutes, we were handed the keys to a 1982 Suburban and told that it was ours for the summer. Within seven minutes, we were shown where the gas was, and told to fill her up whenever she was empty. Within fifteen minutes, we were given the keys to a large wooden shed housing six ATVs and told to fill them up whenever they were empty. Within twenty-five minutes, we were given two .22 rifles, the keys to the ammunition cabinet, and the instructions to shoot any prairie dog that moved. We were not to shoot them from inside the Suburban. Within thirty minutes, we were in the field directly behind the cabin, practicing. To better aim, we rested our elbows on top of a 1979 Bronco with license plate HMFIC—Head Mother Fucker In Charge. Within forty minutes, we loaded into a 1947 army jeep and were given a quick tour of Trails End. We stopped off at the garage, where we were told that the other 1947 army Jeep was getting a little work done to it. We should have the keys to it by the following week. Right around an hour after arrival, we pulled up to the cabin on Hollow Top Ranch, a cabin in which we would be staying alone. We were shown the grill on the porch as well as the freezer with which to feed the grill. The kitchen was stocked with food. The fridge was stocked with beer. We were told to make ourselves at home for the afternoon and that we would grill steaks at Trails End at 7:00 PM. Afterward, we were to drive into Virginia City to watch the fireworks in the evening. It was a pleasant day. This was a different life!

The dining room at Trails End was just as you'd imagine: small and cozy with hardwood floors and an old fireplace. The chandelier was made of deer antlers, and there was a gun rack on the wall.

"I just love having you boys with us!" said Sherry.

"We can't thank you enough for having us," said Donald.

"It's our pleasure," said Eddie. "This place doesn't get enough visitors. Besides, we're going to get some work out of you. The ranch needs it."

"We look forward to it," Justin replied. "We'll work hard, but it's going to be fun too."

"If you work your ass off, we'll show you a good time," said Eddie.

"Sounds like a deal," I said.

"Are ya'll around most of the time?" Chas asked his uncle.

"We'll be here off and on," Eddie responded. "Off next week to Aspen, but we'll be back a few weeks later."

"Tim and Renee will be here the whole time," said Sherry. "They'll take good care of you."

"They can take care of themselves, I hope," said Eddie, "or else we're in trouble!" This caused a good laugh at the table.

"I want to hear what you boys have been up to," said Sherry. "Chas, are you and Paul just having a blast at Virginia?"

"More than you realize," Chas responded.

"Paul, you going to follow in the footsteps and study law?" asked Eddie.

"I don't know; I don't think so," I said. "I'm thinking of applying to the undergrad business school."

"Justin, does that leave you to take over the business?" asked Sherry.

"I'm not sure," he responded. "About to start next year at Alabama. I don't really see myself as a lawyer, though."

"I don't either," joked Donald.

"How's Georgia, Donald?" Eddie asked.

"Been really fun," he said. "But I'm jealous of Paul and Chas. I'm thinking of transferring to UVA if I can."

"Can't handle them Georgia girls?" said Eddie, with a laugh.

Eddie Wachs is a guy's guy. HMFIC for real. He's not overly tough or distant though, not like some people who think they are HMF. He has no pompous attitude. Eddie is always smiling, always glad to be talking with you. Trust me again when I say that you are always glad to be talking to him as well. He is a man of stories, a man who knows how to have a good time. Eddie knows that the time to have fun isn't over when you grow older. It's never over, in his book. He lives the life. The dream. The goal.

Because of that, Eddie does things you wish you could do. He once let the air force train its pilots on one of his old planes in exchange for a ride in a fighter jet. Yet he didn't just ride in the jet; he flew it. Eddie used to race Indy cars. You can't just "race Indy cars." You've got to know about cars. You've got to know about racing. Eddie is one of those guys who knows these kinds of things. In Montana, he gets his adrenaline rush in his plane—buzzing his neighbor's buffalo. Ted Turner has a lot of buffalo. Everyone is a neighbor in Montana. Anything you can dream of doing, Eddie did over twenty years ago. But he's not trying to be the only one who did them. He is extremely generous. We were very lucky to be in his service.

The man travels in good company. Sherry, his beloved wife and the sister of Chas's mother, is his perfect match. Whatever Eddie is dreaming of, she's up for it. Sherry will have just as much fun as he will. They are very much in love. Their looks are quite different, but their warmth is the same. Eddie is on the shorter side, enjoys his meals, lost his hair a good while back, but he makes that sort of look look good. Sherry stands about the height of Eddie, stays in good shape, and has a slim face weathered by many grins. When they stand beside each other they make sense—not because of the way they look together, or even because of similar expressions. It's something deeper, more innate, that just tells you that these people are *supposed* to be next to each other. You want to linger in their company. Over the summer Eddie and Sherry would split their time between the house in Chicago, the ranch in Aspen, and the ranch in Pony. This would sometimes leave us alone on the ranch for weeks. We would await their return anxiously. The best times were not when we were on our own; they were when we were with the Wachses.

Speaking of guys' guys, Eddie's copilot and right-hand man, Todd, is another one. These types stick together. Todd is more reserved than Eddie, but he carries an aura that pronounces his authority in simple fashion. He is one of those guys who wears a mustache to cover up the dirt on his skin. He flew helicopters in Vietnam. His helicopter saw action. His helicopter was shot down. Todd is the guy in war movies that you want to be. He is a stud. He goes just about everywhere Eddie goes. He walked into Eddie's favorable line of vision and knew not to block the light. These two were our inspiration. They were not locals, but Montana men. They knew the land and how to live there. We hung around them to learn as much as we could. When they left, we felt alone, isolated from our motivation.

Of course, we were never truly alone on the ranch. The ranch manager and his wife, Tim and Renee, lived there permanently. They had eighteen thousand acres to watch over! Tim grew up in Montana; Renee grew up in Wisconsin. They both had farming in their blood. I forget how the hell they met each other, but they did somehow. Tim and Renee shared in the responsibility to keep up the ranch. Every day was a workday. They took part of Sunday afternoon off to relax. That seemed to be it. As far as Tim could remember, he had worked every day since he was a kid. They lived the routine. They controlled it. Well, I guess nature itself controlled the routine, nature and Eddie Wachs, that is, but Tim and Renee held the reins. In fact, Tim held the reins to our days entirely.

Man, we hated those reins. Hated that alarm. Even worse than the alarm, Tim's insistence on knocking on the door every morning. Some days we thought, *Maybe he just won't need us today*, but every morning came the knock.

"You want us to do *what?*" Justin asked Tim one morning.

"Climb in there and clean out the dead rats." He must be kidding.

"You serious?" I asked.

"Hell, yes, I'm serious," he said. "Starting to stink up the place."

There was a crawl space above the ceiling at Trails End. Apparently, it was infested with rats, and Tim wanted them out. He figured he might as well have us do it instead of paying for an exterminator. The opening to the crawl space was about three feet wide and two feet tall. If we were to complete the task, we would need to hold the flashlight in our teeth while we crawled on our stomachs, searching for rats as we went.

"I'm off to rake the fields," said Tim. "Make sure you get all the way in there, most of them are along that back wall, I think." With that, he walked out of sight, leaving the four of us staring blankly.

"Fuck this," said Justin. "Hudson, get in there."

"Fuck that," I replied. "Chas, this is your uncle's ranch. You get in there."

"Hell no, Houser, make yourself useful for once," he said.

"I'm not sure if Houser can climb up there," said Justin.

"Fuck you," Donald replied, "Give me that flashlight."

Justin knew the best way to make Donald do it was to piss him off. Donald stood on the ladder and took a peek into the crawl space. He put one knee on the ledge, gave himself a push up, and disappeared inside. He was back twenty seconds later.

He ripped the dust protector down from his face and said, "Fuck ya'll. This is bullshit."

Those rats are still in there, as far as I know. Tim never confronted us on it, thank God. Perhaps he never followed up to check our work, but that's highly unlikely. Maybe there weren't even any rats inside in the first place. Perhaps Tim just wanted to make us sweat a little.

I don't think Tim ever learned our names correctly. Chas would step down from the tractor to, "Nice work, Don." Donald would finish a layer of paint to, "Nice work, Justin." We disliked each other at first. He knew we were pathetic little city kids who'd never worked a real day in our lives. We knew that he knew that, and that he would work us hard simply because of it. But by the end we respected each other. We began to understand each other. I will say that he is a damn good ranch manager. Without Tim around, we would have done about as much work in a month as he had us doing daily. Fences got built. Houses got painted. Fields got cut. Things just got done. The days were beautiful, though. Rise at 7:00 AM. A bowl of cereal on the porch as the day began to take shape. A morning duty until noon. Burgers at the Harrison diner. An afternoon duty until five. A beer from the fridge and a couch. Sunlight until 10:00 PM. Fishing. Driving. Exploring. Cool mountain air after dark. A game of pool at the Pony Bar. Every day was different. Every day was the same. It was wonderful.

"Nancy, make it four Budweisers, please." Nancy was the bartender at Pony Bar. She was about forty years old and had lived in Pony her entire life.

"You boys back again?" she said. "Can't get enough of that pool table, can you?"

"Can't get enough of seeing you," said Justin.

"Now I know you're lying," she replied with a grin.

"Just nice to get off the ranch for some fresh air," I said.

"Now you're really lying," Nancy said. "If you call this fresh air, I'll trade you for the ranch."

"Sounds fair," said Donald. "Do we get the jukebox?"

"I'll even throw in some barbecue," she replied. "You boys hungry?"

"Yeah," said Chas. "We'll take four plates."

As Nancy walked into the kitchen, we made ourselves at home. You could find us there just about every night. In fact, we visited so much that the sheriff drove by the ranch one day just to check with Tim that we were of legal age. Apparently, one of the locals thought we looked a little young, which we were. But Tim stood up for us and vowed we were okay. You see, Tim couldn't have us in trouble with the law; we were needed in the field.

"What do ya'll think of moving out here sometime?" asked Justin, as he struck the cue ball.

"We live here now," said Donald.

"I mean I'd like to live out here for a while, not just a summer," he said.

"I hear you," I replied. "We're gone in a few weeks, and I'm just settling in."

"It'd be nice if there were some girls around," said Chas.

"Yeah," said Donald. "I love Nancy, don't get me wrong, but I'm looking forward to seeing some girls our age again."

"If you had a girl here, would you stay?" asked Justin.

"I don't know," said Donald. "The winter would be brutal."

"Not with the right girl," said Justin. "She could make you a little fire and warm you up,"

"I could do it," I said. "Run a little bed-and-breakfast like the folks up the road."

"You're in love with that girl, aren't you?" asked Chas.

"Think so," I said. "Think she loves me too," I said with a laugh.

"Too bad she sleeps with her fiancé," said Justin, with a bigger laugh.

"I heard about this couple that moved to Argentina," I said. "They run a fishing camp. The guy takes 'em out fishing, and the girl runs the lodge. Heard she's a great cook, too. Now I could handle that."

"Hell, yeah," said Chas. "We could all handle that."

"Ya'll ever thought about taking a year to travel?" asked Justin. "After school, I guess."

"Think about it all the time," I said. "What about moving to Colorado, though? I thought we were doing that."

"I don't know," said Chas. "Could be cool to travel the world."

"You could spend a few months in Australia," said Justin. "Make your way over to New Zealand."

"Couple months in Asia," added Chas, as he struck the cue. "Could go to Fiji and Thailand." The eight ball rolled into the corner pocket.

"Damn," said Justin. "Good game."

"I want to spend some time in South America," I said, as I took a sip of beer. "Been craving to live in Argentina or Chile."

"Hell, yeah," said Justin. "Ever seen the *Motorcycle Diaries*?"

"No," I responded.

"Heard it's about a motorcycle trek through South America."

"Now, that would be cool," said Donald.

"Count me in," said Chas.

We seemed to have the same conversation night after night. What a great conversation to repeat, though.

10

A Different Way of Life

It's a little odd stepping into a legend. You're not sure if you're really there. I stepped into it slowly. I had to keep my balance. Things were moving faster than I expected. Besides, it's the Madison River. You can't just jump right in. You owe it something. Respect. You have to treat it fairly. You have to take the time to recognize what exactly it is that you are doing. I mean, it is the Madison River. It is the life. The dream. The goal. The mama. And she's beautiful.

The Madison was only thirty minutes from our house. For those of you who don't fish, thirty minutes is a stone's throw. It's right across the street. From my point of view, we *lived* on the Madison.

The more you fish, and the more fishermen that you come to know, the more you'll discover that people really are haunted by waters. They will drive hours to spend minutes at a stream. This may seem odd. One of the things you have to recognize is that the drive is part of the fun. The drive to a river is never a bad drive. You think about where you're going. The drive home is never a bad drive either. You think about where you've been. You've got to think about these things.

My first drive to the Madison was made alone. I liked it that way. Another thing you have to understand about fishing is that it is similar to the first time you drive up to a ranch to live there for the summer. No matter how you do it, it is nice. It is nice alone. It is nice in company. Each trip is like seeing the ranches you pass that might be yours for the summer. They are perfect. The times you are with friends—perfect. The times you are on your own—the same. My first drive to the Madison was made alone. I liked it that way.

The water was moving faster than I had expected. It came around the bend with force. I didn't have a clue how to catch a fish there, not that I really cared if I caught a fish. I was fishing in the Madison. I was in Montana, standing in a river as the sun began to set, looking across a prairie at the Bitter Root Mountains. That's all that truly mattered.

Yet I moved on from that moment, eventually. I cast my line upstream only to find it at my side in seconds. I cast my line across the water only to find the rod in line with the current immediately. I cast my line downstream and caught a fish! No, I caught the weight of the river pulling against my line. I did this for an hour. I changed my bait to a nymph. Another hour. A dry fly. Finally, I put my baby on the line. My last resort: the infamous. It is large. It is black. It is fluffy. It has a golden tooth. *What is he talking about?* The woolly bugger!

When in doubt, the woolly bugger. In fact, always use the woolly bugger. Forget dry flies. Forget nymphs. Use the woolly bugger. You will catch *something*. Whether it's a fish, a branch, or a tire, you will catch something. You know that when you tie it on. Of course, you aren't really fly-fishing anymore. You don't get into the smooth rhythm that defines the sport. You have to swing that woolly bugger out there. No more flick of the wrist. We're talking jerk of the arm. A minute later there's a tug on your line. *Always* a tug on the line.

A real one this time! Eight inches. An eight-inch trout. Most fishermen don't even consider this a fish. To me, this was the most beautiful trout I had ever seen. If you think I cared for one second that he was eight inches, you are sadly, sadly mistaken. I was standing in the Madison River. I had caught a fish in the Madison River. Have you done that? I hope so. It feels good. When I said I didn't care about catching a fish, I lied. Now I was content. Now I could go back to fly-fishing. Fly-fishing is so much more enjoyable when you aren't worrying about catching fish.

There was a knock at the door one morning, and I assumed it was Tim, as always. I got out of bed to make sure everything was all right. We weren't late yet, but you never know.

I was surprised to see Eddie standing at the door.

"Morning, Eddie. Excuse me, you caught me in bed." I said, shamefully embarrassed.

"We didn't hire you boys to sleep all day," he said. It was about 7:15 AM on Saturday morning. I couldn't tell if he was serious or joking, but I'm pretty sure it was a little of both.

"Get your asses up, boys," Eddie said with a smile. "The planes are just itching to get some action."

"Planes?" Chas asked Eddie, as he hit the bottom stair, obviously just barely awake.

"Ya'll hungry?" he said. "Nice morning out; thought we might take the planes to get ourselves some breakfast."

You don't usually take planes to breakfast. At least, I don't. Maybe some of you corporate types do on occasion. Not me. Usually an adventurous breakfast is a drive to McDonalds, maybe even a drive to the local joint. We *flew* to the local joint. Well, it wasn't exactly *our* joint, but we flew there anyway. Eddie was bored of cereal on the porch. So we broke out the planes.

When you're in a plane in Montana heading to breakfast, you want the detour. We could have flown to Ennis in about five minutes. That would have been boring. We needed to look around for a while. We headed up into the mountains, over high-altitude lakes, over logging sites, winding our way toward town. It was the best drive to breakfast I've ever had! When we landed at the airstrip (a grassy alley behind the Main Street storefront), we parked the planes directly in back of an old lodge. Breakfast time! We were no further away from the door than you would have been if you'd parked your car. That felt a little odd. It felt like we'd parked on the sidewalk. Most of the planes were parked at the end of the runway. Eddie calmed our nerves. "It's okay to park here. They get mad, but I own the airport." I recommend starting your day that way, whenever possible.

After the bacon-and-eggs excursion, when we landed back at Trails End, Justin bolted out of the plane.

"Sweet!" he said, as he stepped down from the plane. "I flew us home. Did ya'll fly?"

"No shit?" asked Donald. He had flown back in the other plane with Todd.

"Well, not the whole way," Justin replied. "But most of it."

"Got ourselves a natural pilot," said Eddie, as he looked over at Justin.

I didn't mind because I'd flown before, but I sensed envy in the others. Justin had flown Eddie's plane. Eddie loved Justin. He had taken an immediate liking to him. It was enjoyable just getting the chance to watch the two interact. They were like father and son. Now this seemed to make Chas a little jealous—Eddie *was* Chas's uncle. While standing on the runway, I noticed Chas looking at Eddie, trying to get his attention, but Eddie was looking at Justin in admiration. The jealousy was subtle and never acknowledged, but as far as I could tell, it was always a factor when Eddie was around. You see, both Eddie and Justin have that quality—that hands-on, "I can fix it, I can ride it, I can fly it, I can do it, and I *will* as soon as you stop telling me how and just hand the damn thing over to me" kind of quality. I've said it ever since. I think Justin should work for Eddie. Of course, that would mean Chicago. But it would also mean Aspen and Pony. I don't think it would ever work out. We're all pretty tied to Atlanta. But it would be perfect for him. I loved watching them interact.

The breakfast, as is its nature, was only the beginning of our day. We then drove down to the cabin from the runway and broke out the ATVs. With the gas tanks full and ready for use, we headed up the trail, until we crossed into the national forest. The ranch bordered the national forest, which was nice. After a good hour's ride, we reached the site. We had passed over the site on the way to breakfast. This was a ways from the ranch, so I knew we were deep in there. What exactly were we doing?

"Timber!" The yell echoed down the hill and across the valley. I'll say it again. "Timber!" We weren't just cutting down a tree or two. We were deep in the national forest, thinning them out. Tree down, here. Tree down, there. "Timber! ... Coming down! ... Here she comes!" We were logging. Not for some paper mill. Not for some new highway. For our ranch. For our fences. It felt good. At least, it felt good at first. Then we realized our role. *We* weren't logging. Tim and Eddie were logging. We were *dragging*. We were *lifting*. We were *heaving*. It was terrible! For some reason I had glorified the fact that we were going logging. In fact, we all had. We felt like men. Like Montana men. *We're going logging*, we thought with pride. That didn't last long. *We're going logging*, turned into, *If I hear that damn chainsaw whine one more time, if I have to drag this damn log one more foot, if I have to heave one more log onto that truck, I might pretend to be the next needed tree.*

Hours later Eddie concluded that the truck was full. That wasn't a decision he came to on his own. When he tried to fit more logs on the truck, they just started falling off. There was no more room. We tried again, to no avail; the truck was full. In our view the truck had been full about fifty logs earlier, but that was only our view, and it didn't count much. If you need to build a fence any time soon, drive to Pony and stop off at Trails End. I guarantee you there are plenty of logs left over.

Before unloading the forest back at the ranch, there was something that we needed to do desperately—eat, drink, sit, rest, recover, slow down, hold on; we needed to catch our breath. No place better for that than the Harrison Diner. We ditched the ATVs for the Suburban and took off toward town. Not much was said on the long, straight road into town. Too tired to be conversationalists, we just kept to ourselves, stared out the window, and waved at everyone we passed. You always wave at everyone you pass. And they wave back. It's just something you do in these parts. It's one of reasons you live in a place like Montana. Little did I know it was an art form.

Does art imitate life or does life imitate art? In my research I ran across an article entitled, "The Art of the Wave or Always Wave to Art," by John T. Flynn. Now, either everyone in Montana has read Mr. Flynn's article and started waving because they thought they were supposed to, or the wave just comes with the territory. Art imitates life, I assure you. I'll let Mr. Flynn explain.

"A short drive down any roadway in Montana will almost certainly result in someone waving at you ... a failure to wave can be such a breach of etiquette as to label you a stuck-up snob without you ever having uttered a word. The lack of a wave can also be the barometer of the seriousness of a rift with a neighbor. If you have had your differences to the point where he no longer waves, you know the affront was serious and that amends have to be made."

This is an intricate sport and culture. Driving down a road in Montana without knowing what you're getting into can be like driving down the wrong side of the road in England. If you don't know the rules, you will see facial expressions in the locals that you've never seen before—expressions you don't want to see.

If your burger doesn't taste good enough, go logging for a few hours and come back to it. It will taste better, especially at the Harrison Diner. Damn, that was good, so good that the silence continued at the table. The extent of our conversation while we waited in deprivation was, "I'm starving," followed by the realization that, "I'm starving," was about as deep as we could get at that particular moment. And once the food came, there was no chance that you'd hear a word. It was like the first two minutes of your Thanksgiving meal before someone feels guilty and asks a meaningless question. The burger was all the companionship that we needed. Chas even broke out the local paper. When someone breaks out the paper at the table, that's about it for the conversation. Yet, it's not a bad sign for someone to break out the paper at lunch after doing ranch work all morning. He's just tired. It is a bad sign, and I hate to see it, when an older married couple reads the paper in silence at breakfast. You don't ever want to get to the point where there's nothing to say in that situation. You don't want to be that kind of tired.

Not much happens in Montana. Read the newspaper and you'll discover that quickly. The more you read the paper, the more you will find out that only two topics are covered in a Montana newspaper, local politics and trout—primarily trout. It astonishes me that the people of Montana have not tried to elect a trout for governor. Think about it. I'd vote for a trout if I lived in Montana. A trout is the perfect candidate. It represents the majority interests of the population. It is slimy. What else do they want? I don't believe much else. They've come quite close to it, but never quite put the final piece in place. And I quote a local magazine: "Traditional policy changes seem small compared to the latest problem—discovery of whirling disease in the upper Madison River. This highly contagious parasitic disease attacks trout, especially rainbows and cutthroats, with the deadliness of Michael Crichton's alien *Andromeda Strain*. Unlike more traditional problems, this one won't wait for session after session of legislative debate and compromise. Trout fishing is of incalculable value to Montana, its image, and its economy. All concerned interests must move together now on this and other critical issues that threaten our trout heritage." People listen to that type of thing in Montana. Forty-five percent of all adult Montana women fish. Seventy percent of the men fish. Isn't that shocking? Only 45 percent of the women fish? Only 70 percent of the men fish? And they live in *Montana*? How can you not fish if you live in Montana? Many years ago, Ennis had a sign at the edge of town that tallied the population. The trout outnumbered the humans by about ten million.

To celebrate its twenty-fifth anniversary, in 1995, *Montana Magazine* did a special called "25 Years in the Montana News" that ranked the top-ten news stories of each year. Not much happens in Montana. They proved my point for me. I put together a list of my own. I weeded out that list and came up with my Top Ten New Stories of The Top Ten News Stories of Twenty-Five Years in Montana. These are the most interesting headlines I could find. Keep in mind that these are the most interesting stories from *twenty-five years* in the entire state.

1. (1976 #9) Montana State University Captures National Football Championship

2. (1991 #9) Livingston Woman Convicted of Arranging Rape of Her Daughter

3. (1973 #2) Slaying of Four Persons at a Dude Ranch and Subsequent Manhunt for Eighteen-year-old Eagle Scout

4. (1988 #9) Saga of the Richard Kurt Marijuana Farming Operation

5. (1987 #2) Two California Prison Escapees Die in a Shoot-out after a Six-Day Manhunt around the Gates of the Mountains Wilderness

6. (1991 #1) Prison Riot Results in Five Inmates Dead

7. (1973 #10) Trial and Hanging Sentence for Two Young Men Accused of Murdering a Hardin Jeweler

8. (1971 #6) Hijacked Air Canada Jet Landed Twice at Great Falls

9. (1992 #4) Two Military Transports Collide over Northern Montana

10. (1989 #4) Freight Train Explosion Rocks Helena

These need a little commentary:

1. What? How the hell did that happen? Was there a national outbreak of Vicadin that year that didn't quite make it to Montana? Please explain.

2. Are you kidding me? Was this one of those families where all of the cousins are married?

3. A Boy Scout did this? I heard Kazinsky used to lead a group of Boy Scouts.

4. Letter to the Editor: You don't happen to have directions to Old Man Kurt's farm by any chance, do ya?

5. I thought the only thing that happened in the Gates of the Mountains Wilderness was a large fire. MacLean's book *Young Men and Fire* doesn't tell you that more than one thing can happen there. I don't buy it.

6. Inspired by the state of Montana's budget committee.

7. People were sentenced to hang in 1973?

8. The hijackers must have had polarized glasses.

9. You'd be surprised how many planes collide over Montana if you look into it.

10. I didn't know Guns 'N' Roses added Helena to their tour that year.

Those are my top ten. To balance it out, I've also come up with the worst ten. Now keep in mind: these *were* part of the top ten to Montanans.

1. (1972 #9) Agriculture

2. (1979 #10) The Economy

3. (1973 #7) State Workmen's Compensation Division

4. (1975 #7) Agriculture

5. (1985 #4) Montana Weather Swings from Bitter Cold to Heat and Drought and Back to Bitter Cold

6. (1982 #7) Rate Increase for Gas, Electric, and Telephone Service

7. (1979 #1) Rail Service

8. (1990 #7) Public School Finance

9. (1993 #10) Montana Caught up in Dispute over Grazing Fees

10. (1994 #6) Prison Chief Resigns after Dinner out with Female Inmates

Montana is a greater state for the lack of things that happen there. In fact, I wish less happened there. What if the Montana newspapers dropped the local politics and *only* focused on trout? Would that hurt the newspaper? Would it hurt to have no news but trout news? The paper would become a sportsman's guide. I think that would *help* the paper. Then it could go national. Then it could go global! I'm willing to bet *Field and Stream* sells a few more copies than the *Helena Gazette*. Would they really lose that much if they dropped the politics? You can't drop the politics in Washington. You can't drop the finance in New York. But could you drop them both in Montana? Why not? People only flip over to the stream reports anyway. I think there's a reason. I think the politics are a decoy. I think Montana's non-fish-related activities are entirely one large, deceptive decoy.

What if everything that is not fishing in Montana is only there as a façade? What if it is only there to convince outsiders of a false truth—that some things actually matter other than fishing. Why? Think what would happen if the truth were unveiled. Think what would happen if people discovered that Montana *is* only about fly-fishing. People would no longer plan trips to Wyoming. Parents would no longer plan trips to Idaho. Children would no longer venture to Colorado. Everyone would flock to the Mecca. Think about the horror. People would be everywhere. The Madison would lose even more of its isolation. Orvis would be at every intersection. Madison River Outfitters might follow the same tragic path as Abercrombie and Fitch. No, the politics are there for a reason. You need the politics. You need the façade.

Can you believe there's not a fly-fishing store in Three Forks, Montana? Isn't that beautiful? Three rivers merge into one, and there's no fishing store? Nowhere to buy bait? Nowhere to buy tackle? We were played for the fools that we truly were. I had envisioned the store during our entire drive over. The simple dark green hat embroidered with the perfect stitching. The gray shirt that merely wore "Three Forks" on the front and the thin drawing of the rivers' paths on the back. I pictured the guide: a short, terribly skinny man in his forties, with a thick brown beard, and hands reeking of the prey. Then there was my question, "What's been hitting lately?" followed by the response, "What hasn't?" But my fantasy was shattered by the impossibility that no one has opened their doors to the fishermen. No one has trapped the money of the outsiders. Because where there is a fishing store, there is a restaurant. Where there is a restaurant, there is a hotel. Where there is a hotel, there are tourists. Three Forks is far from a tourist town.

Three Forks is Lewis and Clark country. The area was of key importance to their trek and discovery of the West. As you recall, Lewis and Clark were commissioned by Thomas Jefferson to explore the West and document all that they found. As an alumnus of the University of Virginia, which was founded by Thomas Jefferson, I find it comforting that Lewis, Clark, and I shared in a portion of Jefferson's dreams. Mr. Jefferson would enjoy knowing that I made the trek from Charlottesville to overlook the three forks of the Missouri. He would embrace the fact that much of my personal education has been spurred by a self-inflicted passion for seeing a part of the world his eyes have only read about. He would even delve into the depths of jealousy. The land that I find myself transfixed upon is, in fact, west of the United States as Jefferson knew it for the majority of his lifetime—until, of course, he changed all of that. His intention was greater than that of most.

It is safe to say that a small minority of the University of Virginia's students have seen the banks of the Missouri at Three Forks. It is also safe to say that Jefferson would consider any period of time spent on those banks of great value. So, here I am in his shadow, in the silhouette of his shadow rather, attempting to shed light on this land he envisioned.

11

Paradise Lost

Talk about paradise lost! I mean, I was there. Trumpets were blaring. This was the place of dreams. Paradise. I had arrived. I couldn't believe I had actually found it. It was about time. I was beginning to get pissed. In fact, on the way there I kept asking myself, "What the hell am I doing this for?" But I got there. And I didn't expect paradise. I knew it would be good—but not paradise. So you can imagine my concern when I lost it.

Where did it go? It was just there, but then it was gone. The picture remained in memory, but each step seemed to take me further from its setting. Light reflected in harmonious patterns. Dependable ripples stirred the velvet sea. Yet it was gone. I was lost—not just from paradise. I was seriously lost. Each turn failed me. Each step led me further into the abyss. And then I took the turn I regretted—the turn that led me to the steps of death itself. Imagine the horror. When I looked up and saw the Grim Reaper staring me in the eyes, I knew it was over. "So this is it," I told myself. "This is how I'm going to die." My heart skipped a beat. But he didn't charge after me, for some reason. He just stood there, staring into me. And then he did something amazing. His stare slowly began to fade, and then he spared me. In a moment, his eyes passed over me, as he looked down and went on with his business. Now was not my time. I walked away unscathed. I was alive. These are the feelings that arise when you're alone in the woods and encounter a moose. Trust me.

So, I was alive. That was nice. Yet, I managed to get over that fact quickly. I was still lost. Maybe I wouldn't be alive much longer, regardless of the moose. I needed to find the trail. But it had disappeared. One moment it was clear; the next it was gone. Don't try to follow a trail through a large field and think you know where the trail picks up again. At the end of the field each opening in the forest appears to make sense. Each passage looks like your destination. If you find yourself feeling pretty sure that *that's* the right direction, or that it could be *that* one, or maybe the other, don't follow the path. Turn around, and find the trail you arrived on. I didn't. I trusted my instincts. My instincts don't know shit about direction. Within minutes, my senses failed me. There was only one useful point of reference. I knew not to walk toward the crumbling stone that was settled at the bottom of the peak. I hadn't climbed a pass to get there. But all other directions seemed valid. As I turned away from the mountain, in search of a familiar sign, the desperation began to sink in. I was in the middle of the Montana wilderness without a jacket, without a watch, without a compass, without a map, but *with* a four-weight fishing rod. *With* a woolly bugger. Nothing else could have gone wrong, but then it did. The sky darkened in a matter of seconds. And then I felt the raindrop. Then another. Then more. And then the rain began to drown the remaining breath in my soul.

Talk about paradise lost! Compare that moment to the one when I found it. I was on the way up the never-ending trail, alone in responsibility, in search of something else. Well, I wasn't alone in the responsibility of the task, but alone in seeing it through.

The others knew I would do it alone. In fact, I knew it myself. I thought I wouldn't mind. How difficult could it be? The map was so simple that I memorized it. I left it at home. No need for it anyway. It was a nice day. The sun was shining in true fashion. Besides, I could use the exercise. What could go wrong? Hike up the path until you reach a lake. Follow the path above the lake. Continue around the lake on the path. Walk until you reach the second lake. Find the place where the lake drains into a stream. Turn the wheel to close the dam. Stop the stream. Conserve the water. Please the government. Reduce the risk of forest fire damage. Keep the emergency source full. Turn around. Follow the path. Walk back to the first lake. Catch rainbow trout. Walk back home. It didn't seem like a bad day to me. I didn't mind doing it alone. In fact, it was nice to get away.

It was nice until the task got harder. It was nice until the path split, and I had to choose a direction on my own. It was nice until I began walking in uncertainty. For at least a mile I headed up the trail, unsure it was the right one. That was not enjoyable.

"A little further, then I'll turn around."

"There's no way this is it."

"What lake? I'm still climbing up a damn mountain."

But then, a sign. Brighter sun behind the trees. Fewer and fewer branches with each step. I was nearing a pause in the elevation. I began to sense it. I began to feel it. I even found myself jogging toward the light. Tired. Jogging. Breathless. Running. And then I saw it—clear blue purity intentionally isolated from the surrounding peaks. As I neared the banks of the lake, distinct thoughts penetrated my disbelief. "This is paradise. Like nothing I've ever seen before. This is the place of dreams." The closer I got, the better I felt.

I know where the fountain of youth is. And the beautiful thing, the part they don't talk about? It has fish in it! Rainbow trout! You can't imagine this place. It is beyond thought until you see it. It is so beyond thought, that I made an unusual promise to myself that day. *As soon as I get back from my task, as soon as I return from the second lake, I'm going to do something quite odd ... I'm going to go swimming ... naked. I have to*, I thought. *This is the Garden of Eden. They didn't wear clothes there, right?* So, neither would I. All I had to do was find the next lake. All I had to do was turn one little wheel, and I'd be back within minutes. My clothes would be ashore. Not a soul for miles. Forget catching the trout. I would *swim* with the trout! It would be glorious. This was one of those inspirational internal moments that you rarely feel. But there was a problem.

I never found the second lake. I never turned off the water. The Montana government entrusted us to do so. The Wachses, as a favor to the government, agreed to monitor the dam. They agreed, because the second lake is a large source of the water which the Wachses use on their ranch. They agreed, because the hike to the second lake passed by paradise. If the government got hold of paradise, who knows what would happen? Actually, I take that back. I must admit that without the government's protection, many of our enjoyable spaces might be lost. But I understand why the Wachses would want to keep this place as secret as possible. They do a damn good job. I couldn't even find the place before getting completely lost. Now, granted, I didn't take the map, but the map was simple—I'm sure it would have helped, though.

My naïve, blatant disregard for my own personal safety was the larger reason I failed. The no-rain-jacket, no-watch idea was a mistake. Why? Because I didn't have time to swim naked in the lake! That was the problem! I didn't even have time to fish. I didn't have time for anything besides getting home safely. You see, the sky darkened immensely with the rain. Without a watch I had no reference of time. All I knew was that I had spent most of the afternoon hiking miles and miles into the forest. I thought it was nearing night. I thought I had an hour to make it off the mountain and back to the ranch. Getting lost had taken up too much time. I had to get back. With a watch I would have known that I did have more time. Even if I didn't get to swim, I could have at least searched longer for the dam. Instead, I departed with my tasks incomplete—all of them.

Paradise changed on the way back down. Paradise was no longer the lake. The lake looked much blander under cloud cover. Besides, the rain drops on the lake hid any sign of rising fish. No, paradise took on a new form. It was much thinner than the lake. It resembled a stream more than a lake, a tiny stream without any water. The *trail* was now paradise. Finding the trail was far better than my discovery of the lake itself. It's amazing how much paradise is weighted by mindset. The concept of paradise evolves and changes with our needs, desires, and circumstance—it is neither fixed nor permanent in nature.

Tim closed the dam the following morning. It really *was* urgent that we conserve the water. It was not a good thing that the stream ran free that night. Terrible forest fires scorched Montana that year. A drought didn't help the cause. I'm starting to understand why some of the top-ten news stories in Montana involved the weather. The weather has extreme consequences there. The most obvious consequence is the effect it has on collective mindset. Collective mindset is determined by many things, but the quality of the fishing determines it most—that and the skiing. If you live in Montana, you like precipitation. Precipitation means snow. Snow means skiing. Snow means tourist dollars. Well, snow also means shoveling, but skiing and tourist dollars far outweigh any pains resulting from the shoveling. Snow also means melting. Melting means water. Water means fewer forest fires. Water also means full rivers. Full rivers mean better fishing.

We had terrible fishing. I caught a few fish in Montana that year—a few, as in *two*. The rivers were low. The water was warm. I am an awful fisherman. Two plus one doesn't equal ten. We had much better luck when we fished with friends in Sun Valley.

We had friends—Brooks King, Beau Terrell, and Porter Hill—who knew how to time the river. Even though rivers keep time themselves, it's nice to know how to read them. These friends knew how to grab a burger, play a game of pool, drink a beer, and then drive to the river ten minutes before the hatch started each night. They were wiser than us in that regard. I'd never seen a true hatch before. One moment the air above the river was as clear and crisp as you would expect Western air to hover before nightfall. The next, miniature flies covered the water like predators. The flies swarmed with new viscosity that made the canyon look like a glass full of oil and water. When your vision could only discern three distinct layers in front of you—the water, the flies, and the air—you knew you were witnessing a hatch. Precise lines can be drawn between the layers. Sun Valley redeemed my self-esteem immensely. There's nothing like fly-fishing to spoil your self-esteem. That's why you shouldn't demand to catch fish when you go. If that's all you're looking to do, then you are likely to be miserable. You are also likely to be a miserable fly fisherman.

But, as I mentioned earlier, I don't mind not catching any fish. I primarily just enjoy the fly-fishing. I enjoy the rhythm. Yet, we didn't need the rhythm of the river to guide our days completely. Montana has its own rhythm entirely. We had the long Montana days. We had the evenings at the Pony Bar. We had each other. We had the Wachses. We had Tim and Renee. We had the work. We had the circles.

Not much happens in Montana. That's the beauty of it all. Granted, some things do happen, but not the kind of things you're used to. Not the kind of things that itch your comfort. Different things.

Not much happens on a ranch especially. Well, things happen, but you don't really notice them. That's the goal. No one tries to *change* a ranch. All you try to do is keep it the same. A ranch is in its perfect state from the beginning. That's what attracts us to ranches. I guess it is true that a ranch is initially burdened by the fences we build around it. The ranch would prefer that the fences were never built. But as the rains pour down on the fences and slowly weather their rusted souls, the fences eventually become part of the place. At that point, even the ranch itself starts to love its own fences, like a father looking after his son. So, you have to keep up the fences. You have to keep up the land. You have to keep up the animals. It sounds easy, but it is damn hard work.

Paul in front of the Trails End cabin (Pony, Montana)

Donald and Paul in the Trails End barn

Justin on an afternoon break at the ranch

Justin and Chas boarding the plane for morning breakfast
in town

Justin and Chas working the field on Hollow Top Ranch

Donald, Chas, Paul, and Justin on an evening drive to Sun
Valley

Paul and Justin at Trails End Ranch

Todd and Justin on afternoon target practice

Beau Terrell, Brooks King, Justin Rainer, Chas Smithgall,
Paul Hudson, and Donald Houser in the mountains above
Hollow Top Ranch

PART III

Europe

12

The Cinque Terra

The following year, I returned to Europe. This time, the plan was to stick around for a while. I was there to study. Well, not really. That was my excuse. I was there to live in Europe. I was there to meet new people.

For six weeks I lived in Innsbruck, Austria, while taking classes at the university. If you've heard of the program, or know of others who have studied abroad, you are probably assuming that it was one giant party. I'm not going to argue with you there. I was no different from everyone else. We weren't there to learn in the classroom. We did take some classes, sure. Yet the point of the venture was to live and travel in Europe. We were there to continue our education in youth along with that in the classroom. The two types of education are on par in my book. Who wants to look back and realize they missed out on being young? You're only young once.

Out of coincidence, I essentially began and ended my trip in the same locale. Justin and I flew to Europe with my parents before heading to Innsbruck to start the program. We spent three nights on the Italian coast, the Riviera. At the end of the summer, this just happened to be the same place everyone from Innsbruck wanted to go as well before flying home. On my part, there were no regrets about returning. In fact, it seemed quite symbolic. Let me start at the end.

I must say that Monterosso was much more alive. Six weeks earlier it had seemed quieter. Perhaps only because each face had been a stranger's. Perhaps because we were merely stopping through on our way to the next town. But now the faces were familiar. The inflections made sense. The laughs were identifiable. It was perfectly fitting that we would spend our last weekend underneath the Riviera's sun. After all, in a sense, this was where my trip began. Not actually *in* the town of Monterosso, but not far from its path. If only the others could have started there as well. Then they could feel it too. Then they would understand the importance of the full circle I had made. Of course, we had all made our own circles in some manner. Mine just happened to be physical as well as emotional. The tangible nature of the circle aided in the emotion, sure, but it was not entirely necessary in order to grasp the significance.

While the locations we each visited and directions we each took had drastic consequences on our individual experiences, the path didn't always determine the destination. We all reached a certain mental destination in some form or fashion. And who's to say one form or fashion is better than another? Of course, I will. But I'll recognize that, had I chosen other paths, I would have felt equally as strong about this as well. That's how I know paths didn't determine destination. That's how I know elements of everyone's final thoughts were one and the same.

The wine didn't hurt the process either. The wine complemented our conversations. It brought out the taste in the stories upon which everyone reflected. That's great wine. The wine was also *made* in Monterosso. I don't care what you say—if you're drinking a bottle of wine in the place where it was made, it's a great bottle.

The days truly were beautiful. They weren't spent hiking from town to town as I had spent them previously with my parents. There was too much wine to drink to keep us active in that manner. We did travel by sea, though. If there's one thing I can recommend, it would be to do the same, and in a similar style of boat. There's nothing in the world like riding from town to town in the Mediterranean in a four-man wooden structure.

Now, no matter how you approach the town of Vernazza, it will appear spectacular. The view from the trail is breathtaking, to say to the least. From afar, Vernazza bears strong similarities to the geographical shape of Italy itself. It sits at the base of a mountain falling steeply into the sea, yet, at the shore, a large Italian boot juts unconventionally into the ocean. The boot provides protection to the small rocky bay for which the town is known. Aside from the view, the trail itself is breathtaking as well—literally. I didn't know vineyards were so difficult to hike through! I'll venture to guess that most aren't, but when they are perched on steep slopes, as these were, you find out quickly that rich Italian food doesn't in fact put you in better shape than you were before the visit. Perhaps that's why the first sight of Vernazza is so spectacular. Maybe you just can't wait to sit down in one of its patio cafés to rest. So, it's nice to arrive by sea. In conclusion, it is better—especially in a four-man wooden boat, of which we were captains.

What surprised me was the number of people who didn't want to get in the boat, who didn't want to see the other towns. There were a number of our friends who were content to stay in the same spot on the beach the entire day. In fact, they had sat in the same spot the day before—not that it was in any way a bad spot. The beach *was* a nice place to spend your day. But why would you stay in Monterosso if Vernazza was only a short distance away? We were back in an hour. The same humor was even in the air when we returned.

There were those who didn't even *see* Vernazza. That baffles me.

I'm not trying to take anything away from people spending time on Monterosso's beaches. How could you do that? In fact, I had one of my best moments in Europe on that beach.

Here I was on the Italian coast, with both new friends and old, the number of recent memories of foreign cities too many to recall. The sun was shining down. I had consumed entirely too many drinks for the time of day. A group of us sat below a large orange and green umbrella. We relished the shade, focusing on nothing but our weak portable speakers. They shouted Jerry Garcia and David Grisman's

The Pizza Tapes as loud as their "little engine that could" would allow. I decided to take a stroll.

The shops were small, but crowded. Italian voices filled the air. I was inspired. After casually wandering the streets, sipping on a beer, I had a distinct thought shoot through my mind. Here I was, across the Great Pond, twenty years old, taking some of the best steps of my life, both metaphorically and literally. I returned to the group and confessed, "I'm having one of those moments." You know what I'm talking about. The good kind. I have a mental picture of myself *in the moment.* Do you have a picture of *yourself* in moments? I hope so. The best picture is still up here, though. Man, I want to go back to that summer.

Six weeks prior to this, the four of us had walked down the crowded aisle and made our way into an empty room at the back of the train. As we waited in anticipation of movement, travelers with backpacks fit for the likes of elephants or camels kept awkwardly walking past our room. Everyone we noticed appeared to be on an adventurous trek. This is a sight you see often in Europe. It is a sight that I enjoy, of course.

Justin and I were with my parents. We were merely along for a leisurely excursion through the Italian countryside. The ride from Rapallo to the Cinque Terre would take less than an hour. My legs seemed to stretch themselves as thoughts of the afternoon surfaced. I looked up to see a young woman, probably in her late twenties, heaving her backpack onto the shelf above us. She took a seat in an exhausted manner that silently announced that the rest of the train was full, and that she felt lucky to find our hidden company. I knew the Cinque Terre was a popular spot. I did not know that it had become the traveler's theme park for which we now appeared to be waiting in line.

After long minutes of stillness, I noticed a discrepancy between the schedule and the time on my watch. One becomes accustomed to this in Italy. I finally felt a small nudge as the engine pushed us out of the station. We were off. My parents were sitting directly across from me and Justin. They gazed out the large window at the ocean. I could see the enjoyment in their eyes at finally feeling the rewards of months of planning. Their eyes were relaxed and smiling. I remember the notion settling quietly upon me that this would be an afternoon to remember. I was with three of my best friends in the world—my father, my mother, and Justin—and we were about to spend the day exploring the Italian countryside. My father broke the silence by asking the young woman beside him if she was going to the Cinque Terre as well. Her response baffled us all.

"No, I'm actually on the way to Venice."

A subtle smirk appeared on Justin's face. I must say I felt the same way. It would take a hell of a long time to get to Venice on *this* train. We were on the local. It stopped at almost every town along the track. Her next statement drove us into a frenzy.

She said, "You know you're on the train to Rome, right?"

I'm sorry, could you repeat that? Rome? Our faces were horror-stricken. The tide had turned. A subtle smirk now appeared on *the woman's* face.

"You're not on the wrong train, are you?"

Yes, my dear, we are.

"Do you know when we're supposed to arrive?" my father asked.

"It only takes four hours. This is the express train."

"Four hours!" my mom shouted.

Our day was shot. We would have about enough time to buy a postcard of the Coliseum before catching the train back home. I'd seen Rome. I wanted to go back someday, but not now.

Luckily, even express trains make a few stops, probably only for travelers like ourselves, who board the tube in London expecting to see the Eiffel Tower when they "mind the gap." The first stop, our desperate chance to take Marley's advice to "stop that train—I'm leaving," was in the town of La Spezia. We were actually only about a thirty-dollar cab ride from Riomaggiore (part of the Cinque Terre). I could think back and try to remember the price in lira, but it will surely be a figure in the high thousands that carries no meaning to most people. Riomaggiore was one of our planned stops. The day wasn't shot after all.

Riomaggiore is the easternmost village of the five coastal fishing towns that make up the Cinque Terre. We had intended to arrive by train at the westernmost town of Monterosso, approximately eighteen kilometers away from Riomaggiore—that is, until we joined the crowd heading to the seven famous hills of Rome.

The birth of Riomaggiore dates back to the eighth century, when it was founded by a group of Greek refugees who had escaped religious persecution.

I'll venture to bet that the romanticism in the air dates back to its first discovery. It is a nice place to walk around, although quite hilly.

Each of the five towns in the Cinque Terre is connected by footpath. In one blistering day you could hike to all five if you liked, granted you had taken it easy on the wine the previous night. Our intentions were to arrive by train in Monterosso, hike a few of the legs, and then take the train to the others. The plan was reversed once we found ourselves walking down narrow streets of pastel houses at the other end of the line.

We began walking through the many levels of Riomaggiore: down stairs, down roads, down anything we could find to get us to sea level. We were searching for the start of the "Via dell'Amore" (The Lover's Pathway), which starts in Riomaggiore and walks along the coast to the next town of Corniglia. The Via dell'Amore is the easiest of the Cinque Terre's paths. It is not the easiest to find.

"Excuse me, where's the Via dell'Amore?" I asked one of the shopkeepers.

"You're not far." You're never far in Europe. "It's just down this road here."

Once the suggested road ended, with no sign of a trail, round two of questioning began.

"Excuse me, where's the Via dell'Amore?" I asked again.

"You're not far. Take these stairs to the bottom. Take a right, and you are there."

This goes on for half an hour. No sign of the path.

At last we make a wrong a turn and *accidentally* end up at the trail. I knew this would be an afternoon to remember. The entrance was thoroughly blocked off by a large wall that must have been constructed weeks before.

"Construction. Landslide Damage. Trail Closed."

Turns out the trail had been closed for a month. It also turns out that Italians are about the least helpful people I've ever met. The people at our hotel spoke of the wonders of the trail. They even asked if we were going to hike to all five towns. There's a slight chance, although very slight, they hadn't heard that you couldn't hike to all five towns. The trail was closed. You couldn't have completed the hike for quite some time now. I'll grant the hotel naivety. But the locals in Riomaggiore?

"Excuse me, how do we get to the Via dell'Amore?"

"You're not far. It's just down this road here."

"You're not far. Take these stairs to the bottom. Take a right, and you are there."

The locals even wore smiles as they gave the helpful directions so unselfishly. What did they think we were trying to do, take pictures of the Trail Closed sign? Not a single person thought it relevant to mention, "By the way, you know the trail is closed, right?"

The envisioned day had become an organizational disaster. Of course we *were* still on the coast of the Cinque Terre, which *did* turn us into uncaring, hopeless romantics. So, the day itself was far from lost, even though we were. Forget improvising. We would just start over.

We made our way to Monterosso, via our second unexpected cab of the day, to start where we originally intended. We finally arrived at the "first stop." We put the past behind us and began the day as planned, although a few hours behind schedule.

The trail from Monterosso to Vernazza was apparently actually open. We felt the need to buy something before we departed. You haven't really visited a town unless you purchase something. You need that exchange with the locals, even though brief, in order to get a sense of the place. We wanted something refreshing, but perishable. I wasn't about to hike to Vernazza with a replica sculpture tied to my back.

"Four Cokes, please," said my father.

"I'll have a Diet," my mother casually corrected.

"Make that three Cokes and one Diet Coke."

We settled for the usual Coca-Cola. The fact that it was readily available soothed us a great deal. As you recall, we are Atlantans. We're proud Atlantans at that. Pepsi signs make me cringe, especially in Europe. If you like Pepsi, you must be a misguided soul. Or, let me rephrase that: you must have misguided taste buds. I believe there are help groups willing to work with you. My advice is to go to one tomorrow.

After admiring the people wading in the shallows of the Mediterranean, we walked through the tunnel beneath the medieval tower of Aurora in search of the path. Upon following difficult directions, we finally reached the base of the hike.

"Feels good to stretch the legs," said my father as we walked around a bend, the view of Monterosso disappearing behind us. "This trail is pretty famous."

"I'm just glad it's open," said Justin.

"Work up an appetite," said my mother. "We've got a nice dinner tonight at the hotel."

An hour later, I found myself walking next to my father, as we hiked through the rolling vineyards. Mom and Justin were just up the path, chatting away about how Justin's mother would have loved to have been with us.

"How's work been?" I asked.

"Pretty good," he replied. "Been busy. I've been working to get some new clients lined up, which has taken up a lot of my time. Should be a good year, though."

We have this conversation about once a year. My father rarely mentions work around the house. When he leaves the office and comes home to my mom, they talk about everything in the world they can imagine, except work. It is a great trait to have. Work should be work and that's it. One should put every effort into it during the day, but at the end of the day one should put it aside and enjoy the comforts of home.

"You ever think about retiring?" I asked.

"Paul, I don't know what I'd do if I retired," he said. "I love golf, but not enough to play it every day. Think I'd get bored. And I love the law. I enjoy going to work in the morning. Keep that in mind; it's important to love what you do."

"I could retire tomorrow and keep myself busy," I replied.

"I know you could," he laughed. "Wish I had some of your creativity. What would you do if you could retire tomorrow?" he asked curiously.

"Probably open a recording studio," I said. "After I took a year off to travel."

"Well, keep dreaming like you do, and one day it'll happen," he said. "Just remember to always set goals. You can't reach any goals if you don't set them first."

Our afternoon's adventure, which truly turned out to be just that, ended in Vernazza. Getting lost had taken up too much time. We had to get back. We had dinner reservations that we were not about to miss.

Hotel Splendido is a nice spot for a meal. The hotel was the first stop on a ten-day trip that my parents were taking to celebrate my mother's birthday. She likes to celebrate her birthday on more than one occasion. She says she deserves more than just one day. She does.

A reminder: Justin and I were only in their company for these initial days before departing for our six weeks of study in Innsbruck.

To say that Hotel Splendido was a nice place for our last meal on the Riviera is quite the understatement. In fact, it is well known for being a nice place for just about anything. Splendido is owned by the prestigious Orient Express Group that owns more than its fair share of the world's finest hotels. The Cipriani in Venice and the Lodge in Vail are other elite hotels with the same recognition.

My father determined that Justin and I were not of an age to sleep there. He asked the Splendido to find us another hotel nearby that was better suited for boys in their twenties. They must have misheard his request. Our hotel was neither nearby, *nor* better suited for boys in their twenties.

We stayed in the town of Rapallo. This is two towns away, I might add (one would have done just fine), which doesn't make for casual rendezvous. We loved it. Splendido arranged for us to stay in the nicest five-star hotel in Rapallo. It seems Splendido must be quite arrogant to believe they were putting Justin and me in the squalors, as my dad had requested.

The dining area at the Splendido sits on a large elaborate balcony, which looks over the town of Portofino. The town lies hidden from the Mediterranean in its own personal cove. Call it The Cove of Royalty, The Cove of Perfection, The Cove of Hidden Beauty—you get the picture. It is a nice cove.

Small wooden boats are not parked in this harbor. Hundred-foot yachts are—many of them. Portofino's distinct setting will not be matched by any attempt. Before joining my parents at dinner, Justin and I walked around town, amazed. We weren't alone.

Justin and I had time for a drink at the Splendido del Mare before dinner. The restaurant sits along the square of Portofino, looking out at the harbor. This was surely the correct first step of our night.

"What'll it be?" asked the bartender.

"Two glasses of red," I said.

"Anything in particular?" he asked.

"No, whatever you suggest," I said.

"Any seats on the patio?" asked Justin.

"You can take the two in the corner," he said.

We sat outside and watched the people strolling through the square.

"You talk to Laura today?" I asked Justin.

"Yeah," he said. "Called her while you were at the pool."

"How is she?" I asked.

"She's bummed I'm gone," he said. "She thinks I'm going to meet someone new over here."

"You won't find anyone like her, though," I said.

"I know," he replied, "but she won't listen when I remind her."

As we spoke, a girl who was drop-dead gorgeous walked into view.

"Maybe I'm wrong!" I joked.

"Damn," said Justin. "This place is amazing."

"I can't wait for Innsbruck," I said.

"I know," said Justin, "Been thinking about it all day."

"Not Laura?" I asked with a laugh. "If she knew you weren't thinking about her she'd kill you."

"I know," said Justin. "Don't tell her. What time's dinner, by the way?"

"Now," I said, "we're running late."

We finished our glasses of wine and walked up the hill to the Splendido.

Aside from Splendido's fabulous food, service, and wine, I thoroughly enjoyed being in the company of my parents. Spending time with them will never grow old. In fact, our conversations seem to age with the wine that my father now favors.

"Look at how lucky we are," my dad said at one point during dinner. "It's not often that you get to have dinner in such a beautiful spot."

"Not a bad view," I added with a laugh, as I nodded toward a woman at the table next to ours.

"She can't touch your mother," said my father. "I'm the luckiest man alive."

"Oh Paul," said my mom, "You can't say that *every* time we have dinner." She was smiling, though. My parents are very much in love. "You boys better not settle down with the wrong woman. Finding the right girl is the most important thing in life."

"I think I found her," I joked, as I was still looking at the woman across the way.

"She's too old for ya'll," said my mom.

"Looks just right to me," replied Justin.

Although I was sad that night that my next dinner with my parents would be more than a month away, we were all excited about our upcoming outings. The four of us left the Splendido with much restraint (always restraint when walking *out* of its doors), but Justin and I were looking forward to a night on the town.

The town we chose to peruse was not Portofino. People in Portofino are too drained from admiring their view to stay up later than a glass of dessert wine or a cup of decaf Italian roast. The town we chose was not Rapallo either. After many attempts the previous night, we had discovered that there was absolutely nothing to do in the later hours there. By process of elimination, we ended up in between the two locales, in Santa Margherita.

Just as Monterosso is more open to the sea than its nestled neighbor of Vernazza, so are Santa Margherita and Portofino. They are distant cousins of a sort, although not that distant, unless you board a train to Rome. In the Riviera, it seems that the larger the view of the Mediterranean, the more lively the nightlife. I guess that shouldn't come as a shock. What other inspiration do you need for a drink than vast views of historic water? Someone described Santa Margherita as, "aristocratic and elegant, intimate and familiar." They forgot to mention that the women, who are *all* gorgeous, were our other inspiration for joining the wee hours of the night.

Santa Margherita is apparently quite a famous and historical little spot.

Justin and I decided to have a drink. The drink definitely changed the course of the night, but I'm afraid to say it left no mark on history.

It was unfortunate that the two of us were not fluent in Italian. It would have been nice to speak the language with the company around. On second thought, it might have been even better that we were American, as we seemed to be drawing attention. Yet this would have only been true if we could speak enough Italian to make the women think that our accents were cute. But we realized that you do not need to speak Italian in order to drink Italian beer. This was a nice consolation.

It was not to our benefit at the time that the last bus returned to Rapallo at midnight. It was also not to our benefit that a cab would have cost upward of thirty or forty dollars, possibly fifty, since we couldn't speak Italian.

We were going to have to make the trek on foot. Besides, as you recall, we had been prepared earlier that day to hike another trail. Why not postpone it until the early, early morning?

It seemed like the right time to head home at 4:00 AM. The walk back was going to be the world's longest drunken stumble. This was not a very safe idea—especially considering there was not a sidewalk. We stalled.

You can imagine our excitement when the last bar in town had an open door and had the lights on. We needed to rethink our decision over a beer. A small Guinness sign greeted us upon entry. We raised the attendance from three to five. It didn't take long for Justin to share our situation with the others. They managed to come to a rather quick conclusion.

"Why walk to Rapallo now?" one said. "It will take you hours."

"How else are we going to get there?" asked Justin.

"The first bus starts running at 7:00 AM," said the bartender. "You might as well just take that."

"You'll get home at the same time," said another.

Bartenders have always been the world's disguised geniuses. But what were we to do with hours to spare?

"What time do you close?" Justin asked.

"We're open as long as you're here." Good answer.

The Italians were utterly fascinated by the concept of a car bomb. They thought we were literally insane. Now, a *car bomb*, you might say? What exactly were you two up to? We weren't plotting to destroy the city at dawn; we were plotting to destroy ourselves immediately.

A car bomb is a drink. People like to set lofty goals. The car bomb is a direct result. How does it work? Take a pint of Guinness. Take a shot glass of Bailey's. Drop the Bailey's from the shot glass into the Guinness. Drink it as fast as you possibly can. That is a car bomb. Maybe we *were* insane. Who has the right to make that call? I can't say it's not fun, though! We received a round of applause at completion. We received a second round upon request for another beer. I doubt we left a pleasant impression on the first-shift bus driver. When we got back to the hotel, Justin tried to call long-distance to Laura. The Italian operator apparently knew how to say the phrase, "You're too drunk. Go to bed." I tried to tell him the same thing.

It's amazing what can happen underwater in the Mediterranean. For starters, your hangover vanishes almost entirely upon entry into the water. I'm not sure what else happens there, but the hangover part definitely makes it worthwhile! Needless to say, we were late to meet my parents at 10:00 AM for the boat they had rented. I surely owe them something for our irresponsibility. Hopefully, my family will make it back to Portofino, and *I* can be the one to treat. I need a shot at the Splendido as well.

13
Lost in Italy, as Usual

"Don't get on the wrong train," said my father, as we walked toward the station. "Do you want me to stay? I can help you get on the right one."

"Dad, after yesterday? The last thing we have to worry about is getting on the wrong train."

"Your mom is crying in the car."

"We'll be okay. So will you. Your trip is going to be great."

"I'm jealous of yours."

"We'll call you when we get there."

"You've got the numbers, right?"

"Yeah, I've got 'em."

"I love you, Dad. Have a great trip."

"I love you too. Don't get on the wrong train!"

"Bye!"

"Bye!"

As my father was almost out of sight, I yelled, "Dad, tell Mom I love her."

"I will. Ya'll be safe."

Justin and I sat leaning against our oversized backpacks, as we waited for our ride out of the city. Our trip was about to begin. You knew it by looking at us.

I overheard a young American man behind me telling a group of teenagers to stay close, that the train would be here soon. I walked over.

"Excuse me," I asked.

"Hey." He turned around.

I continued, "Are you guys going to Milan?"

"Yeah, we are. Is that where you're headed?"

"Yeah. We got on the wrong train yesterday. I'm trying to make sure we don't do it again. These trains aren't marked too well."

"I know. No one's very helpful either."

"I've noticed."

"Well, you can follow us. Our train should be the next one."

"Thanks," I said, feeling reassured.

Sitting with the other Americans on the train would have been an obvious and unneeded sign of weakness and dependence. Justin and I settled into our own car, sure that all we had to do was watch the landscape until our arrival. The train made a few local stops at first. Then I knew the brakes would get some rest as the conductor pushed on to Milan. My next sight caught me a little off guard.

"Justin? Aren't those the Americans?" I said, as I pointed.

"Where?" he asked. He looked out the window. "Oh, yeah. Why?" They were hustling toward the station.

"They're going to Milan."

"Really? Why'd they get off?" Our eyes figured it out together. They locked in a panic. *Why else would they get off?*

"Oh, shit."

"*Perdon*," I said to the passenger across the aisle. "Does this train go to Milan?"

"Milan? No, this is the local."

"Shit."

The train began to move again.

"Shit!"

"What do we do?"

"I don't know, get off!"

"Now?"

"Not *now*. At the next stop."

"How the hell do you get on the right train?" Justin was stating the obvious.

"I don't know, but we're not on it."

"Where's our damn train?"

"It's got to be the next one behind us."

"Why the hell did we follow that guide?"

"I don't know. He was a tour guide."

As we complimented Italy on its simple, easy-to-follow transportation, the train began to pull into Genoa faster than we'd expected.

"Shit, we better get off," I said.

I grabbed my bag off the rail, and ran toward the door. I looked back, and Justin was right behind me. The doors were open when I reached them, and I jumped down onto the landing. No one jumped down behind me. I turned around to see the doors flying shut in Justin's face. *Oh, shit.* I saw through the glass that Justin muttered the same. He looked at me with a blank stare. In a frantic moment I mouthed out, "I'll stay here," as I pointed toward the ground with an oversized gesture. His lips mouthed, "Okay."

It wasn't until I took a step back that I realized the depths of my situation. The train had departed. No one else had gotten off at the same stop. It was nearing dark. Then I turned around. I could see over the walls of the outdoor station into the neighborhood that surrounded me. I was in the slums. The streets were empty. The houses were boarded up. A sole traveler stood on the opposite side of the track, yet, not a traveler, but a homeless person. Rational fear overcame me. I was alone in the slums of Genoa, miles from Rapallo or Portofino, separated from Justin, and we had missed our train.

I walked to the edge of the station. I wanted to be in the closest spot to first sight of the next train behind us. I parked my bag beside a worn bench. A train appeared in the distance. As it approached, it was not slowing down. When it rattled through the station I caught a glimpse of the word *Milan* on the front of the first car. *Shit!* Even if Justin and I *had* been together we would have missed our train. The Milan train was an express train. It was not about to stop in the slums of Genoa. No one within miles of where I was standing was heading to Milan.

I noticed a major problem. Trains coming from the other direction were not stopping either. *How the hell is Justin going to get back here?* I thought. That notion didn't go away. I waited for thirty minutes before a train stopped from Justin's direction. No Justin. I felt desperation approaching much more rapidly than any train I had spotted.

At last I heard voices at the other end of the landing, feminine voices. When I looked up, I noticed two young women approaching. They were apparently dressed for a night on the town elsewhere (*naturally*). The girls stopped about fifteen yards from my bench, likely scared by my desperate appearance. They were speaking Italian—of course they were. There was no possible way for me to ask for help. I didn't even know what help to ask for, yet I wanted help somehow.

But wait, I realized. Maybe I *can* ask for it. *This* Italian was different. This Italian was somewhat more familiar. Then it hit me. They weren't speaking *Italian*; they were speaking Spanish. I know Spanish (sort of).

I walked over.

"*Perdon.*" Excuse me. "*Se habla ingles?*" Do you speak English?

"*No. Habla espanol.*" No. We speak Spanish. "*Se habla espanol?*" Do you speak Spanish?

"*Si, un poco.*" Yes, a little. "*Me llamo Pablo.*" My name is Paul.

"*Me llama Cecilia. Este es mi amiga, Francesca.*" My name is Cecilia. This is my friend, Francesca. Francesca nodded. Cecilia appeared to be the talkative one. The fact that I could communicate in any form or fashion surprised me. Perhaps it was better that they spoke Spanish. My English self was too scared to talk. It was better that I speak in broken phrases. That's how I would've communicated in English anyway, so I at least had the disguise of a foreign language to cover that up.

"*De donde eres?*" Where are you from?

"Soy de los Estados Unidos." I'm from the United States. *"Soy de Georgia. Soy de Atlanta."*

"Somos de Ecaudor. De Quito."

I responded, *"Quito? Sabe Quito."* I know Quito.

"Sabe Quito?" They seemed surprised at my answer.

"Si, yo visite Ecuador por un … ah … como se dice 'mission trip'?" Yes, I've been to Ecuador for a … how do you say, "mission trip"?

"No se. Pero, sabe Quito?" I don't know. But, you know Quito?

"Si, Quito es mi amor."

"Tu amor!" Quito is your love! (My Spanish is excellent.) *"Adone vas?"* They asked me where I was going.

"Ah … Voy al Innsbruck. Voy al Austria."

"Austria?"

"Si. Austria. Pero, tengo una problema." Yes, Austria. But there's this thing … see, I'm by myself in the middle of the freaking Italian slums without my friend, without any clue of what I'm doing. I'm lost as shit. Help me! Help me! Help me! Please! (I didn't say that word for word, but that's what I meant by *problema*).

"Austria? … una problema? Cual es su problema?" You're going to Austria? You're obviously in the wrong place, buddy. What the hell are you doing here?

"Si … ah … no tengo mi amigo … ah … no sabe adonde voy." Trust me. I really am lost as shit.

"Paul!" *What?* I spun around. Justin was standing behind me.

"Justin!" Where the hell did he come from? Then I saw that a train that I hadn't noticed had actually stopped.

"We missed the damn train to Milan," he told me.

"I know. Wait … how the hell did you get back here?" I asked.

"On that damn train," he said, looking down the track.

"I know, but how did you get it to stop *here*? I thought you were gone."

"I know."

"I thought we were on our own. I thought I'd see you in Innsbruck … maybe."

"I know. My train didn't stop for like three more stops. I had to ask someone how to get back here."

"How *did* you get back here?" I was still baffled.

"I saw the name of the town when I left. The next train back wasn't for half an hour. I thought you might have left."

"I know. I wanted to." I can't tell you how glad I was to see Justin.

Justin agreed. "This place is a dump. I saw a car on fire when I pulled in."

"I know. I almost wigged out. Thank God you're here. How the hell are we going to get to Milan?"

"Milan? Neccesite ire al Milan?"

"Wait. Who's this?" Justin asked. The look on his face was hilarious.

"Este es … I mean, this is Cecilia."

"Who's Cecilia?"

"Sabe Ecuador? Pablo sabe Quito." Do you know Ecuador? Paul knows Quito.

"Paul! What the hell's going on?"

"Sabe Milan."

"I met some friends," I interjected, trying to explain the situation to Justin. "Wait … hold on." Did I hear Cecilia say *"Sabe Milan"*?

"Cecilia, sabe Milan? Sabe como … ah … ire al Milan?" Please! Please! Please tell me you know how to get to Milan.

"Si. Necesitas ire al Milan? Si. Yo sabe. No es una problema."

"Justin, I think she knows how to get there."

"You're going to listen to her? Paul, what's going on? Who is this girl?"

"Justin. Look around. Who else are we going to listen to?" The place was deserted.

"Shit. Okay. Ask her how."

The noise down the track distracted us all. We turned around to see a train pulling into the station; it was stopping. Cecilia seemed to recognize the train.

The only reason that I even knew I had fallen asleep was my recognition of the feeling of waking. I couldn't have slept for long, although the shade on the window appeared to have a glowing ring around it. A few streaks of light shot between a crack in the shade, as the train made a steady turn to the left.

So, I was right; it was light out. It had been dark the last I remembered. As my eyes began to adjust, I looked across the cluttered room to an interesting sight. There was an old man, probably in his sixties, snoring with his mouth wide open, his head only a few feet from mine, as the aisle between us was far from wide. There hadn't been anyone across from me the last I remembered. Train travel doesn't claim to be personal or luxurious. At least not this train; this train began in Italy and we all know by now what to expect of Italian trains. Yet, I must give the Italians some credit. Even though Justin and I had to sit for three hours in the aisle before any space opened up in the sleeper car, at least someone made the train wait for us!

You see, Cecilia *did* know what she was doing. She and Francesca led us to the central station in Genoa (which they weren't going to), hurried us toward the ticket room, ordered us tickets to Milan (we didn't trust ourselves to do it at that point), and sent us on our way with surety. They even helped us carry our bags as we ran through the station in search of the departing train (at which point it hit me that Justin and I could've easily had our bags stolen). Maybe Italians would've stolen our bags if we had been in Rome being helped by the city's many "innocent" children. But not Cecilia; she was pure. We even exchanged numbers before jumping on board (I bet Donald gets some interesting phone calls). In hindsight, I should have given her my real number. I should have kept in touch. I wish I could thank her now. I should have at least written her number down instead of merely pretending. But the encounter was meaningful for the moment, even though there was an element of insincerity involved on my part.

When we sat down on the train, Justin looked at me with an unusual look of concern.

"Paul, they really were nice people."

"I know. They didn't have to do that."

"I feel kind of bad," Justin said.

"Why?" I didn't think we had done anything wrong.

"When she asked me for my number I wrote down Donald's."

"No shit? Me too." *What are the odds?* I thought.

Justin said, "I always give out Donald's number to strangers."

"Me too."

"Really?"

"Yeah. I mean, it's Donald."

"I know. This better be the right train."

"I know. I think it really is this time."

There is nothing particularly nice about the Milan Central Station, but something about it makes the station gorgeous. To start with, it is *huge.* The Milan Central is twice as tall as it needs to be, and twice as wide as that. It's actually a great place to spend a little time, even though there isn't much to do there.

"Tomorrow! We need to get there tonight," I told the man in the ticket window.

"I am sorry, sir. The next train for Innsbruck leaves tomorrow."

"We need to get there tonight!" I wasn't backing down.

"No, you will get there tomorrow, on the next train." Neither was he.

"Is there *no* way tonight?"

"There is *no* way tonight. Excuse me, sir. People are waiting."

"How close can we get?"

"Sir?"

"How close can we get to Innsbruck *tonight?*"

"*Tonight?*"

"Yes, tonight." This guy was starting to piss me off.

"A train leaves for Trento in an hour. You can catch a train to Innsbruck in the morning."

"Okay, how do I do that?"

"How?"

"Yes, how? What train do I take?" Nothing was easy with this man.

"The train to Trento!" he yelled.

"But what train is that!" I don't know what freaking train goes to Trento.

"Trento! Track nine!" Finally, the answer!

"Track nine?"

"Nine!"

"Okay, that's all I needed to know. Jeez."

There's something specific about riding in a train in the middle of the night through Europe. I don't know if it's eerie, comforting, too silent, not silent enough, or what. But it *is* unique riding in a train in the middle of the night through Europe.

The train ride took quite a while longer to get to Trento than we expected.

"Excuse me, sir?" The attendant sealed the open, whistling door as he entered our car.

"Ticket?" he demanded, before I could proceed.

"Yes, here." He seemed distrustful as he handed it back. "How far until Trento?" I asked.

"Trento?"

"Yes, Trento. Do you know how far?"

"Half an hour."

"Yes, I know it is half an hour; it was half an hour an hour ago. How far, though? How many kilometers?"

"Where are you going?"

"Innsbruck."

"Innsbruck?"

"Yes, Innsbruck."

"This is not the train to Innsbruck."

"I know."

"You must go to Trento."

"Yes, I know."

"Half an hour."

"Do you know how to get to Innsbruck from Trento?"

"Innsbruck? Trento? Hold."

The attendant began speaking rapid Italian into his radio. I *did* manage to decipher the word *Innsbruck*, so at least he was paying attention. After a minute or so, his static conversing stopped, and he looked back down.

"Half an hour," he replied and he began walking down the aisle. *Thanks for your help, buddy.*

An hour later he appeared again, this time from the whistling door on the opposite end of the car.

"Next stop," he said as he approached our seats.

Justin and I looked at each other as if to check the other's belief in his instructions. Justin spoke my mind exactly, "Might as well. I don't know where we're going."

Our stop appeared to be a frightfully small town. There was no way in hell we would find a hotel at two thirty in the morning in *this* place.

Justin began walking toward the schedule board. "We better find out when the Innsbruck train leaves. We don't want to sleep through it."

A train was stopped on the other side of the tracks. An attendant stood beside the door.

"Excuse me. Do you know where we can find a hotel?"

"A hotel?"

"Yes. A close one."

"No. Where are you going?"

"Innsbruck. Tomorrow. We need to find a hotel."

"You're going to Innsbruck?"

"Yes. We're going tomorrow. We need to find a hotel. Do you know which train to take to Innsbruck?"

"Yes, this one."

"This track?"

"Yes."

"What time?"

"*What time?*" He was either confused or pissed.

"Yes, what time is the train to Innsbruck?"

"Now! *This* is the train to Innsbruck!" I guess he was pissed.

"*This* one? Not *tomorrow?*"

"No, *this* one. If you go to Innsbruck, get on *this* train."

"We don't need a hotel?"

"No hotel! *This* one!"

"Paul, I think we should get on." Justin jumped in.

"Do you think it's the right one?" I asked.

"Who knows? Maybe they waited for us. Let's just do it. He looks mad."

After I convinced myself that the snoring old man across the car was harmless, I sat up from my makeshift bed and groggily looked around. I attempted to casually walk toward the window to peer around the blinds. Casual didn't last a step. Bags, blankets, jackets, and people were everywhere. I put my foot onto the pile of bags on the floor and shifted my balance upward. Immediately, everything crashed, and I stumbled forward in a cursing daze, bracing myself on the top bunk, the forehead of a sleeping German lady, *anything* I could find for stability. I felt like I was on the damn Mayflower, when my hand finally hit land on the blinds at the other end of the room. Anxiously, yet suddenly frustrated, I opened them to discover that our train was steadily drifting through a large canyon at the base of bright blue sky and towering mountains. My frustration faded at this sight.

"Justin, wake up!" I was elated. I was ready to jump out at the next stop and ask for the longest hike around. "Justin, I think we're in Austria." I was waiting for him to spring down from his bunk and sing "Hallelujah," as he gazed out at the sky.

"Paul," I heard, as he appeared to be reading my mind, "go back to bed!" I guess not. Justin's desperate wail from beneath his blanket quickly reminded me that he was far from a morning person. I think I also heard a "Yeah" from the German lady on the top bunk. I suppose I was a little anxious in my rising. It was 6:15 AM. There was no chance in hell I could fall back asleep, not after I had looked outside and realized that this was what I would soon be calling home ... at least for six weeks.

14
Innsbruck

What a place to call home about! Remember how Denver looks as you drive in on I-70 toward the Rockies? Imagine that you keep driving and get to the center of town. Look up at the mountains. Those in Innsbruck would be twice as tall. Look up at the buildings. Those in Innsbruck would be twice as short; four times as old. Now picture a life-size mirror being rolled in behind you. Even as you turn around, you can't escape the mountains—you are surrounded in all directions. This is Innsbruck. It gets better. Take the Madison River flowing through the Bitterroot Valley two miles west of Ennis. Now place it in the middle of Denver, make the current twice as fast, and call it the Inn River. This is Innsbruck. Take the sky, and make it bluer. Take the grass, and make it greener. Take the time, and make it slower. Take your thoughts, and make them longer. This is Innsbruck. This was where we lived for six weeks. This was our home.

It's important to see a town in both the light as well as the shade. You would be misguided if you only saw the lighter days. You also must see the town from as many directions as possible.

Surely you don't understand Sausalito if you merely eat lunch there and never drive across the Golden Gate Bridge. It is not until you cross the bay and look back at the banks of Marin County that you understand what Sausalito embodies. The same goes for San Francisco. You can't pretend that you know the place if your walk stops in Presidio. This is especially true for your hometown. It is not until you venture elsewhere that you can look back on it with comprehension. Your home is only the intricate center of much broader circles. You've got to see the larger pattern before you can settle down into the smaller one. The last rung of the ring hardly stands firm at the edge of your country. How can you understand the United States until you have driven across the border from Canada? How can you understand North America until you've taken a nap on a nine-hour flight?

Everyone in Innsbruck spends their first day wandering around town. This is crucial; you've got to get your bearings straight. You've got to find out where the streets end up. You've got to know where the tourists eat pizza, where the locals sip coffee. Innsbruck is a great town in which to do that; there is a tram there. It is *always* good to walk around towns that have trams. It is important to know these types of things. Some people have never even gotten *on* the tram. How could you walk on the sidewalk if you didn't know how it felt as you moved past it on the tram? Of course, once I took the tram, I preferred the sidewalk; Innsbruck is a great place to walk around. There is the Old Town with clocks and towers and cobblestone and stores. There is the New Town with banks and apartments and gardens and schools. The first day was spent well amid all the activity.

Yet, the next day, there was a problem. Everyone appeared to want to do the exact same thing as the first day. One day of exploration seemed to be plenty. Yet there was so much more to see. It was the second day that you discovered who knew what they were doing. The second day was sunnier than the first. The first had that type of cloud cover that appropriately told you that Innsbruck was as much of a winter place as it was a summer one. But it was nothing but summer on the second day—bright and blue.

After I spent the morning being introduced to my Introduction to Business Management and Introduction to Music classes, Justin and I walked back to the Rossl in der Au, our local hotel-turned-dorm for the summer. The Rossl sat across the Inn River from the university.

On the bridge, we had a brief conversation with a few of the others whom we had met the previous night.

"What are ya'll up to later?" I asked.

"Probably just going to chill for a bit," said one.

"I heard that Zebra Bar is pretty cool," said another. "Might go shoot a game of pool."

The third friend jumped in, "Think I'm just going to walk around for a bit, check out the town."

"All right; well, maybe we'll catch up with ya'll tonight," said Justin.

As we left the group and neared the center of the bridge, I asked Justin what he wanted to do. Justin's eyes slowly panned across the Inn, above the Rossl, above the valley itself, and into the looming granite mountains shooting up into the heavens.

"Are you thinking what I'm thinking?" he said.

My response was an understanding nod, followed by a simple, "Yeah." You see, Justin and I have a similar eye about things.

There were those who never even ventured into the hills. There was probably someone who never even walked around town. The immense lack of effort that I came across daily, in Innsbruck, of all places, astonished me. How can you live in the city and not go up on the mountain? How do you even know what Innsbruck looks like if you only spend your days *inside* of the town?

Once you depart the gondola at the peak, the setting truly begins to sink in. It seems that in the moment you step out onto the mountain and peer down upon the quiet city, you realize why Innsbruck is there. It is far from *looking up* from the valley below that this knowledge occurs. Sure, it begins there, but you can't let life's beginnings fool you into thinking they are the end. It is the moment you crest the summit and view the unknown world *behind* the mountain that the concept of Innsbruck even truly begins to take shape. You simply cannot enjoy the green valley around the city until you discover the never-ending spires of rock that encompass the mountain range, lurking in the shadows behind it. It is when your eyes draw the lines of the Continental Divide that it all seems to come together. It is when you follow the Inn from the east to the west, follow the mountains from the north to the south; it is when you discover, not one valley, but two, that you understand the presence of Innsbruck's churches and schools.

There are those who never even ventured into the hills. We were there on both the lighter days as well as the darker ones. It is the combination in my memory now that brings me the most comfort. I couldn't appreciate the one without the other.

The social scene on our trip was, in a word, ridiculous. It was the largest density of the most fraternal dudes you'd ever seen. It was frat star central, "coolalogic," the fraternal Mecca of the Western Hemisphere. If you usually thought you were cooler than the guy beside you, this is where you ended up. I'll explain the people in only a few words: University of Georgia, University of North Carolina, University of Virginia, University of Alabama, Louisiana State University, Southern Methodist University, Washington and Lee—you get the picture. And *everyone* thought they were better than the next. So much for being all right. Not here, not now.

I'm going to keep the character development to a minimum; it is for my own personal safety (not because of the stories I could tell—well, maybe, but also because of the time it would take me to tell them). I could spend years describing the people on my Innsbruck trip. I have other things I want to do with my life than getting into the nitty-gritty of all that. In order to do it right, I would have to weave the following people into the story. You'll see why I'm taking a rain check. They are: Hayward, Jaime, Rigdon, Walt, Katz, Russ, Ezell, Elizabeth, Cam, Flinn, Hayes, Lucy, Lindsay, Grady, Chet the Bod, Page, Connell, Gwin, Patty, Emily, Dorian, Chas, Meredith, Patrick, Robert, John, Annie, Phelps, Todd, Monty, Whitney, Christy, Julia, Jeff, Justin, Will, Andrew, Macon, Rachel, Alison, and Susan Joy—and those are just the people I hung out with most of the time.

I'm sorry, but I can't tell you the whole story, not in that way. Besides, the stories are not mine alone. I wouldn't even be the right one to tell them.

So, Innsbruck is famous for its women. This is at least true for six weeks each year when the Americans arrive. *You* may know Innsbruck for the Olympics. The Winter Olympics arrived in Innsbruck in 1964. Regrettably, they returned in 1976—not that the games in '64 didn't go well, but they were supposed to go to Denver in '76. Denver wasn't about it. Denver's voters rejected a five-million-dollar bond issue that was needed to help finance the games. They cited cost, environmental impact concerns, a recent spike in violent hippies, and a sudden fear that foreigners would steal their unfound gold as their primary reasons to give the games the boot. Seriously, those were their reasons.

For all of you fishermen out there, I wish I had some stories from Austria. I *did* buy a custom-made, graphite, four-piece five-weight for ninety bucks in the *one* store that sold fly-fishing gear. You save about $150 when the rod doesn't say Sage on it. The problem is that you can't fly-fish in Europe—anywhere! The Inn sounded like the ideal place, didn't it? My allusion to the Madison was intended to create that feeling. But, in fact, the Inn River is far from the ideal fishing spot. The Inn is deep and strong and fast. The Inn has no rocks, no eddies, no pools; it is just one fast, solid current that you don't want to fall into—at least, this is how it runs through town.

You will probably be arrested if you try to fly-fish in Austria. No, they don't think it is harmful; they think it is *theirs.* The water, that is, and the land. It is theirs. It is European property. Someone owns it. It has been handed down for centuries. It is not just sections of the stream that you avoid because they are on private property. There aren't even any Private Property signs. *Everything* is private property! Think about it. Do you think there are any plots of land in Europe which nobody has discovered yet? Do you think there are still places that people consider common ground? Hell, no. Do you know how long people have lived in Austria? Here's a brief quote that I came across: "Around 15 BC, the Roman Empire expanded forcefully northwards, annexing the central alpine region approaching the

Danube. The area around Innsbruck thus became a transit route of key importance for Roman soldiers." Do you even know what *BC* stands for? It stands for, "Get the hell off of my property and take your fishing pole with you!" In order to fly-fish in Europe you have to obtain permission from the owner. Permission is hard to come by. It is also vastly expensive. Don't get me wrong; there is great fly-fishing in Austria—it is actually some of the world's best. We just couldn't fish it. European fly-fishing is considered a "gentleman's sport." We were apparently *not* gentlemen in Austria.

The Germans appeared to think otherwise.

15
Munich

The presidential suite at the Marriot in Munich—that's where we stayed the first night. How about that for not being gentlemen? We slept on cots, though. Who needs a king-size bed when you can sleep on a cot? Especially when the actual *rooms* of the suite were already rented out. We didn't have the keys. Let me explain:

"Well, there is *one* room left in the hotel. We can give it to you on special rate for only a hundred dollars."

"We'll take it," I exclaimed, amazed that they actually gave us a room.

"I have to warn you though, there aren't any beds there."

"Are you putting us in a closet?" asked Justin.

"No, you'll have more room than a closet. It's actually the living room to the presidential suite. We've rented out the suite's rooms. But the *living room* isn't rented out. We can roll some cots in if you want to sleep there."

Excuse me; did you just say the words *presidential suite*? It's not often that you can trick the front desk into giving four twenty-year-old boys the keys to that place. I couldn't even pull that off at the Motel Six, let alone the Munich Marriot. But my friend Grady can. The best way I can describe Grady is to tell you that he is the kind of guy who can arrange for you and your buddies to sleep in the presidential suite when the hotel is booked solid. He can then take it a step further and convince the hotel that they are royally screwing you over, in order to get a discount.

Do you think we cared for one second that we slept on cots? Do you realize how *big* the presidential suite is? Do you realize that instead of a small room with a fridge, we had a kitchen, a dining room table, three sofas, and a big-screen television? We celebrated immediately.

There was only one place in the hotel that would allow us to celebrate in the style fitting our new presidential mood. Not the bar. Most of our friends went to the bar. We went into the basement—in robes. What's in the basement? The spa. The pool. The steam room. The hot tub. We even ordered room service to bring four Heinekens down to our new throne at the spa. Those were pretty damn good Heinekens!

It doesn't get much better than a Heineken in the hot tub of the Munich Marriot on your first weekend excursion across Europe, after living in Innsbruck, Austria, for a week.

Yet there is a better place for a beer. If you've been to Munich you know it—the Hofbrauhaus. The Hofbrauhaus is a spa in itself. It is a meeting place for all the discontented minds that need soothing. Much soothing seems to accompany a large, heavy glass of German lager. A beer in the Hofbrauhaus is to a Bud Light just as the building itself is to your local bar—five times bigger with twice as much character. The Hofbrauhaus is probably the most renowned pub on earth.

The Hofbrauhaus is a communal place. You don't go there to catch up with a friend you haven't connected with in months. There are no small tables in the corner to do that. There aren't any small tables at all. In fact, you can't sit by yourself if you try. I'm not even sure if it is allowed. You sit in groups, and you sit where you can. If that means that you don't know the person next to you at the table, then so be it; you'll know them much better after the first beer goes down, let alone after you spend the entire afternoon there. To answer your question: yes, people spend the afternoon there.

My first thought upon walking into the Hofbrauhaus on that damp Saturday afternoon was that the only other people inside would be travelers like ourselves waiting out the rain. It did seem like a logical place to do that, being right in the center of town, of course. And what better way to see the sights of Munich than after spending an hour or two in one of the city's finest establishments?

But surprisingly, spending Saturday afternoon in the Hofbrauhaus seems a tradition of the locals. All of the tourists who had been there the night before appeared to be sleeping off their hangovers. To answer your question again: yes, we were there the night before as well. New crowds filled the tables—all of them, literally. Justin and I did three laps inside the building before finding two empty spots on a bench next to an entire German family (grandparents and all). They drank us under the table (grandparents and all). So I take it Germans like a good buzz. At least this is true on rainy Saturday afternoons at the Hofbrauhaus in July. I'd bet this holds true in October as well.

It's not surprising that the National Socialist German Workers' Party (later known as the NAZIs) essentially got its legs at the Hofbrauhaus in February of 1920. What better place to drum up support for an idea than the largest room of drunken people in the city? It comes as no shock that Adolf Hitler managed to rally a crowd of nearly two thousand people into supporting a plan there (by plan, I mean it could have been *any* plan). After a few beers in the place you'd cheer for just about *anything*.

I can picture it now:

"Hey man, what's everybody cheering about? What's that guy saying?"

"I don't know. I think he said something about how the next round is on him."

"Really, what's his name?"

"I think it's something Hitler."

"Hitler? Heil Hitler! Buying us beers!"

I probably could have stood up when I was there and used excerpts from *Walden* to convince the crowd to burn down the English Garden to make room for a new high-rise. I have no point other than to say that if any ridiculous ideas are going to start somewhere, the Hofbrauhaus makes as much sense as anyplace.

I was much too young for a beer on my first visit. I was only thirteen years old at the time. I enjoyed myself thoroughly, since my father began recounting his youthful memories of the place. He told us stories about when he sat at the table as a younger man, drinking the same beer with his buddies. He told us stories about some of their European antics that got them both *into* and *out of* trouble. Importantly, he told us stories.

My dad and his friends had quite the routine down. One night they would stay in a relatively decent hotel to get some good rest and comfort. The next they would spend in the cheapest place they could find, to sleep in a bed but save some cash. Every third night they would literally sleep in their cars, in preparation for the next night's hotel. I imagine they went to the Hofbrauhaus before they slept in their car in Munich (at least I would). I imagine they also attempted to emulate the Hofbrauhaus every third night along the way. I'm glad I know those stories about my father; it's important to know those types of things.

Now, enough about Munich. Let's talk about Paris.

The following weekend, I found myself sitting in front of the Eiffel Tower on Bastille Day, drinking wine, and watching fireworks.

That's another great thing about Europe. Living there allows you to say things like, "The following weekend I found myself sitting in front of the Eiffel Tower on Bastille Day, drinking wine, and watching fireworks." If I were writing a book about my life now, the next sentence might read, "How 'bout them Dawgs?" It's just not the same. It's not necessarily *better*, but it's just nice to have a change of pace every now and then. Everyone should experience the pace of life in Europe. You notice so much more when you slow your run down to a walk and start paying attention to what's around you.

It remains one of the top-five moments of my life. Those don't come around very often. The ten of us sat there in awe—in awe of our view, in awe of where we'd come from, in awe of where we were going, in awe of our lives, in awe of each other. Each brought a bottle of wine. The Brie and crackers were only fitting. The entire city was a roar. The past hour we'd spent rushing through the streets in search of the proper place to behold the anticipated moment. We decided to head for the obvious center of the upcoming enthusiasm—the Eiffel Tower. After finally settling down comfortably at my destination, I couldn't help but stand up every few minutes to simply turn around and gaze out at all of the wonder. My life was amazing at that moment.

Only four nights prior we had been in Innsbruck, celebrating yet another summer evening at the Hoffgarden. Two nights prior, Justin, Grady, and I had fallen asleep in the unusual town of Amsterdam. We took the overnight train on Wednesday to meet up with Donald, Chas, and the girls there. Donald and Chas were on the last stop of a two-week vacation that had begun in Rome. We made the trek to enjoy their company before their nap on the nine-hour flight back home. On Friday morning we said our good-byes and left to meet up with the others in France.

Now, at their sides, we sat in the park, each with a bottle of wine. We sat comfortably in the grass, eating Brie, casually gazing at the Eiffel Tower hovering above us. After we waited for some long, eager minutes—long, eager minutes filled with the air of laughter—the first lone firework shot boldly into the sky, freeing itself from its shell. The condensed eruption announced, with a burst of light and color, the beginning of the night.

It was Independence Day. Bastille Day. July 14, 2001. The first firework usually beats them all. But just as the city began to exhale from this first new breath of the evening, eyes suddenly drifted below the explosions to a wave of light shooting up the face of the Tower. The entire structure was flashing with strobe lights. The Eiffel Tower thus became the primary firework; the night thus had a new star. The sky, the night, the city, the people—all were alive and free.

Here we were, sitting in a park in Paris, with new friends and old, drinking wine, eating Brie, staring upward in awe of the largest fireworks show we'd ever seen, a show that took place directly above a glowing Eiffel Tower. Don't tell me that I wasn't advancing myself in the proper direction in life. Don't tell me that my internship, only weeks before, was of much more importance than *this*. What good is a goal if it doesn't allow you to live? Paris is a great place to do that.

Now that I've expressed the previous moment in full, I must make an important disclaimer: What the hell is all of the hype about? You've got fireworks, music, parades, dancing, the works, but for what? On July 14, 1789, the people of Paris stormed the prison of Bastille to free the oppressed. It sounds valiant, right? That seems worthy of celebration, right? But listen. These courageous French patriots freed an entire *seven* prisoners from tyranny. *Seven*! Do you know how few people *seven* is? One, two, three, four, five, six, *seven*. Hell, Butch Cassidy could have done that alone! Then there's what happened afterwards. Louis XVI recognized the revolt and retreated to Versailles. The French claim that the storming of Bastille was proof that power no longer resided in the King. They claim that power was now with the people and that their monarch ran in fear.

Do you think Louis XVI didn't *want* to retreat to Versailles? Have you ever been there? I'd retreat there every weekend if I could. He probably just wanted to go shoot some quail or something. He was probably just hung over and needed to take a night off. But, *no*, you might say, the storming of Bastille was the start of the French Revolution! The French Revolution was one of the biggest flops in history! Do you know what followed the French Revolution? The damn *Reign of Terror*! "We're free ... oh shit, we're not!" And after the Reign of Terror? Do you know what came then? Napoleon. Sure, he was a bright guy. Maybe you should celebrate that. But don't pretend he wasn't a *monarch*. Don't pretend he was a leader of a *republic*. Do you know when France really became free? It was in 1875. Bastille Day was in 1789. What the history books *don't* tell you is that France was just boring as hell in 1789; Bastille Day only exists because the French really just needed an excuse to party. But they do throw a great party. You should go there if you get a chance.

Perhaps it is fitting that I once walked the streets of Paris. Perhaps it was merely a rite of passage. It appears you can't write a word in the United States until you have strolled across the bridges of the Seine.

What is it about the Seine that does the trick? How does its current cause so much wake? My best guess is the sunset. A sunset in Paris can make a writer of any of us. But something else must happen. Words are up for grabs. Stories are left untold. Each writer leaves a stroke in the stream that is somehow strangely understood by others. Historic works seem to lie in an eddy. The new writers know where the boulders are. The writers know how to move them.

As I contemplated this question, I realized that, in concept, what I'm describing is merely the same as children learning from their parents. As children, we are taught their wisdom. It is up to us to move forward in life. Each child takes the gifts of his ancestors and uses them to cross boundaries. We aren't meant to merely follow in our parents' footsteps; there's so much more. We are to learn their paths, understand them, and then know where the hills are and avoid them. Each child is a compass, each life the straighter line.

16

Paradise Found

A few weeks later, as Justin and I walked the streets of Innsbruck, I asked him an important question.

"Where do you want to go next weekend?"

"I don't know," Justin replied, "Prague?"

"That's where everyone seems to be headed."

"Supposed to be awesome," Justin said.

"I don't know, though," I replied. "I'm not sure if that's where I want to go." Something was on my mind. "There's another place I'm itching to go."

"Where?"

I needed to go back to the place where I discovered what it means to travel. How could I not? It was right around the corner. You don't pass up this place if you can picture it and know how to find it. Of course, I was narrow-minded in going there. Why go to the same beach that you've always gone to? Why not go to a new one simply to watch the waves crash upon different shores? But I'd only been to this beach once, and, dammit, I was going back. This beach lies in the heart of the Swiss Alps.

Murren is a tiny little town that bears such a heavy secret. The views from Murren are not like those of other places. Its views are *much* wider, *much* taller, *much* deeper. Murren peers down on the town of Lauterbrunnen, and apparently down on *all*, all except one. The peak of the Eiger Mountain taunts the little town; in fact, it apparently taunts everything. If you gaze at the Eiger it will admire your respect. If you stare, and stare too long, the mountain stares back, and wins.

Oh, to those who have been to Interlaken and think that they know Lauterbrunnen. Oh, to those who have been to Santa Margherita and think that they know Portofino. You poor souls. If only you'd known what was just around the bend.

There are *only* seventy-two officially recognized waterfalls that grace the cliffs of Lauterbrunnen. You need not worry that people will call you a liar if you run into town having seen more.

What lies beneath such moisture? Vast fields of green pastures—vast fields of green pastures surrounded by 500–800-meter cliffs. What surrounds the cliffs? The Alps themselves. So you have yourself enclosed by pastures, pastures enclosed by waterfalls, waterfalls enclosed by cliffs, cliffs enclosed by the Alps, and the Alps enclosed by the sky. I am convinced that this particular valley is the center of the earth, if not heaven itself.

The beautiful thing about it is that the pastures don't stop at the base of the mountains. The pastures don't even stop in the valley. Rather, they rise with the mountains themselves. Lauterbrunnen is one of the few places on earth, it seems, where you can start hiking in a grassy field up the edge of a mountain and still be in the same field half an hour later. This place defines *indescribable*. To put it in another context, Lauterbrunnen looks just like the town from *How The Grinch Stole Christmas*. That is what it looks like, and those are the people. Haven't you always wanted to go there? Well, you can.

But if too many people visit Lauterbrunnen, will it retain its allure? This is an important question. With each new person who goes to a place, the place becomes less and less what it once was. Should I not even talk about these places at all? Do writers only ruin, and not enrich? Or is there some sort of unique system of life's levers, perhaps divinity itself, which continually keeps it all in balance? Is the harm that I inflicted on these places by visiting them somehow equally weighted by the learning that some might gain through this account? Will the people who intrinsically enjoy my story from the comfort of their bedrooms be moved to exploit what's sacred about these places, by actually visiting them and adding their unnatural element? For each person who buys this book, is there another who's only buying a disposable camera? Can the one happen without the other?

After a long sip of coffee and a moment of deep thought, I have concluded that the writing must go on. Without writing, nothing would change. Without a reason to act differently, very few would. If Lewis and Clark had never written a word, why would you travel to the West? Not until the abundance was discovered did the movement actually begin.

Think about where we'd be without the story of the wagon trail. Think about where we'd be without the story of the Mayflower. It actually goes all the way back to the Garden of Eden. Think about where we'd be without the apple tree. Would we be better off? I don't necessarily think so. Nobody really talks about it, but perhaps we were *supposed* to eat from the apple tree. Perhaps that is part of what we're here for—to eat from it and then learn. How can you understand anything in the world if you don't know what you're searching for?

If no one had gone to the West, we would be stuck thinking that New England skiing was the best in the world. Imagine the horror! Without discovery in general, think what would happen. Nothing would happen! We need to teach those who are unaware so that they can learn and move forward. Why leave what you know, unless you know of something else? Every idea, every discovery, everything would be meaningless unless conveyed to others. How can you convey these things? To start, you can talk about them. You can teach your friends and neighbors with your voice. *The Odyssey* would not exist without voices. But voices fade. How can you convey forever? Writing.

Everything seems clearer now. *The Odyssey* is not one of the greatest works ever written solely because of its content; it is one of the greatest works ever written simply for the fact that it *was* written. The actual writing of the story was the true odyssey, in my mind.

So, while most of the others were in a bar in Prague, I was back in Lauterbrunnen figuring this whole thing out. I told you it was important that I go back there! But I didn't spend the entire weekend in reflection. There was so much more to see. Justin was with me, of course, as well as a few others.

The others knew of something that I did not. To drill the point one last time: in life, it is important to share what we know with others who are unaware.

What I didn't know was that only two hours from Lauterbrunnen there is a town called Nyon. This town is one of the many Swiss villages that sit quietly on the shore of the largest freshwater lake in Western Europe—Lake Geneva. Another thing that I didn't know, and I didn't know this until now, is that all of the towns on Lake Geneva really aren't any different than the towns on the Inn; they are all river towns. But, wait, you say, I thought Lake Geneva was called *Lake* Geneva for a reason? I guess not. The body of water surely appears to be a lake. Yet Lake Geneva is essentially just the widest section of the Rhone River.

The Rhone enters the basin near Villeneuve in the east, which is in Switzerland. The river exits at the south shore, which is in France. The Rhone then gains a beautiful French accent as it travels through France to Marseille on the coast of the Mediterranean.

It is estimated that if you followed a drop of Rhone water throughout its path, it would take seventeen years to cover its seventy-three-kilometer path to the Mediterranean. Most of this time is spent in Lake Geneva—wine country. What a gorgeous spot to grow a grape!

As I said, Nyon is one of the many Swiss villages that sit quietly on the shore of the lake. At least, this is usually the case. The town was far from quiet when we got there. In fact, it was far from quiet the entire time we were there. That should make some sense. We were there to attend one of the largest rock festivals in Europe.

Have you ever heard of the Paleo Festival Nyon? I didn't think so. Here are a few people who have: BB King (1985), James Brown

(1986), Curtis Mayfield (1988), Joe Cocker (1989), Miles Davis (1990), Paul Simon (1991), Jethro Tull (1992), Neil Young (1993), Ben Harper (1994), Bob Dylan (1995), Jamiroquai (1997), Herbie Hancock (1998), Oasis (2000), and the North Mississippi All-Stars (2001).

I didn't know who the North Mississippi All-Stars were. I didn't know what Paleo Festival Nyon was. Damn, am I glad that I found out.

At first we thought that we were the victims of unfortunate circumstance. When we read the sign announcing the concert schedule, we discovered the All-Stars took the stage at 1:00 AM, *not* 1:00 PM as we thought.

It was noon. We were thirteen hours early. It appears we couldn't distinguish between AM and PM in French, or even that it crossed our minds to do so.

"Shall we stay?" Justin asked.

"Yeah," I said. "We can chill at the beach until it starts up."

"Good call," he replied. "Can't believe there is a beach in this place."

I found it better that we spent the day in Nyon. We needed a day at the beach. Contrary to popular belief, days at the beach are quite productive. (Are you by chance sitting at the beach during this sentence? If so, you are very lucky. If so, put this damn thing down, and hop into the water! I'll be here when you get back. I'm not going anywhere.)

So, what is Paleo Festival Nyon? Imagine that when you are born, you fall in love with music. Imagine that when you take your first step, you fall in love with traveling. Imagine that after twenty years of music and travel, you stumble upon a gathering of musicians. Imagine that these musicians are some of the best that you have ever seen. Imagine that they are playing under a large white tent resembling the Denver airport with wings. Imagine that this tent is one of many. Imagine that each tent is decorated with thousands and thousands of lights. Imagine that these tents are in a small town. Imagine that this small town is near a lake. Imagine that this lake is in the middle of mountains. Imagine that these mountains are the largest that you have ever seen. Imagine that everyone is dancing. Imagine that you know *why* everyone is dancing. Imagine that you hear drums. Imagine that you hear guitar. Imagine that you hear a wailing organ.

Why the dancing? Imagine all the people. It's an incredible thing to witness. Not a bad place for a little music. Not a bad place to celebrate life. Not a bad Saturday night.

The following Saturday we sat on the shores of the Mediterranean Sea. We sat in the town of Monterosso. After six weeks of living and traveling in Europe, I had returned to the place where I'd begun my adventure.

We sat drinking wine. The wine complemented our conversations. It brought out the taste in the stories that everyone had to reflect on. My story stood out no more than the others. Each of us had his own stories to tell. Each story was magnificent.

Hopefully, you are eager to go on your own little journey. Well, start planning it. What's holding you back?

All it takes is a little walk down new streets and this book becomes yours, not mine.

Grady Luckey, Clay Rigdon, Chas Strong, and Justin Rainer
in Monterosso, Italy

Justin attempting to get some rest on a train to Budapest

Grady on afternoon assignment for "art class" in Innsbruck

Paul on a hike in the mountains above Innsbruck

Justin in the Lauterbrunnen Valley, Switzerland

PART IV

Lake Tahoe

17
Caribbean in the Sky

So this is it. Part IV. This is the end's beginning. I'm still here. I'm still writing. How, I'm not quite sure, but I've kept with it. This book has become a part of me; it has changed me. I am a new person now. There's no stopping anymore; not here, not now. I want to say that I never thought that I'd make it. I want to say that I never thought that I'd finish. Yet, that would be a lie. But how, or *when*, was beyond me. I remember writing about Aspen and Telluride with such thought and such detail, never knowing when I would ever wake up in Africa. Paris was only a brief, intangible thought, an unidentifiable moment in time lingering in an uncertain window. But I knew I would get here; I knew it the moment I first thought to write. You don't wake up one day and decide to write a book; you wake up and decide that something's got to change. A story *has* to be told. There was nothing uncertain about that.

I began to write, and the more I wrote, the more I realized what I wanted to say. Each night took me further into this newly found addiction. When stories took weeks to tell, and not hours, you might think that I became frustrated. You might think that I persuaded myself that I was attempting the impossible. I have a one-track mind, and who's to say that the thought to write this book was even rational? But this is real, and I understood that from the get-go.

None of these words were written in a drastic setting. I never wrote the contents of my soul in the midst of any certain beauty. I wrote them at a desk. I wrote them at a table. I wrote them in Charlottesville. I wrote them in Atlanta. I wrote them in New York. I wrote them at night. You may have picked up on that, given the tone. I imagine this book would be quite different if I wrote it primarily during the day. But there's too much to do during the day, especially if you have a job that requires attendance.

The last experience I'm going to write about, in this particular collection of stories, revolves around my summer in Lake Tahoe. This was the summer before I graduated college—my last shot at freedom (at least for the time being).

I never wrote a sentence in Lake Tahoe. That may seem odd, right? Wouldn't that be a great place to kick back and write? But I couldn't sit at a computer in Tahoe; that would be illogical. There were other pursuits that I needed to follow.

You see, if I wrote in Tahoe, I couldn't write about *living* in Tahoe. Tahoe is one place that you truly want to live.

Now, I have no doubt that my mind was in a heightened state, digging for words, paths, and answers, while writing. But writing requires that you sit motionless at a desk for hours on end. It is not what I consider living. I needed to get out. I needed to explore. California is such a great part of the country to explore.

I moved to Tahoe to live with the band. Isn't that a great sentence? Being the musicians that we were, we were dreamers. Ideas were what we were all about.

The band consisted of Hunter Jones (guitar, vocals), Will Beights (bass), Ben Hoover (percussion), me (piano, guitar), and Skip White (number one fan).

Hunter and I met early in our first year at Virginia. Musicians tend to find one another rather quickly. We started off as a duo, playing acoustic guitar at fraternity parties along Rugby Road. Yet we soon began to strive for a bigger sound. Will Beights was the next addition. Will was a bass player who went to high school with Hunter in Charlottesville. Beights lived in Richmond, studying the arts, but drove to Charlottesville often. It was worth our while to add him to the band.

Beights was probably the *second* most carefree guy I knew. He was a terrific bass player, which helped, but we primarily just loved his company. Skip White was the *first* most carefree guy I knew. Skip was our biggest fan. He liked to tell everyone that he was our manager. We told everyone that as well, just so Skip would stick around.

Ben Hoover was the last to join the band that year. Ben grew up in Virginia Beach, on the coast, and was a year behind Hunter and me in college. Ben was our percussionist. Growing up at the beach seemed to force the rhythm into him—perhaps the waves had something to do with it.

A few others also lived with us: Vandy, Scott, and Jimmy. Friends from Charlottesville, they had heard that we were getting a place in Tahoe. The three drove out to Tahoe under the assumption that they would get a second cabin nearby. Yeah, right. As you can imagine, that second cabin never happened. Eight of us ended up living in a three-bedroom place. Everyone was a native of Virginia, except me. And of those from Virginia, everyone was a native of Charlottesville, except Ben.

Donald, Chas, and Justin were not able to break away, due to internships and summer school. I was left to spend the summer with a new crowd. Although I was going to miss the usual crew, I was excited to be off with the Virginia boys.

As we pulled out of the Brownsville gas station in Charlottesville the morning of our departure, I turned my stereo to track five. There was a certain song that I needed to hear, a certain song fitting for our departure—fitting because Hunter and Ben wrote it. It's a simple song. In fact, there is only one verse. This verse summed up our collective mindset:

I hear there's gold out in California; I hope what they say is true.
There's too many roads, too many miles,
To get all the way out there and say that we're through.
Oh, California; oh, Sierra Blue.
Oh, California, I pack my bags and we're through.

At our first stop that day, after a good four-hour stint, we pulled out the map in West Virginia. We needed a pretty large map to cover the distance between Charlottesville and Tahoe; there's a lot of space in between, in case you haven't noticed. How far had we gone? How long was this actually going to take us? To get an idea, we pulled out our ruler (the arm of a pair of sunglasses). We had gone about as far as the Costa del Mar emblem.

So we kept driving along. After crossing the South Fork of the Shenandoah River, the Maury River, the Greenbrier River, the New River, the Kanawha River, the Guyandote River, the Big Sandy River, the Kentucky River, the Ohio River, Pigeon Creek, the Wabash River, the Little Wabash River, the Skillet Fork River, the Big Muddy River, the Kaskaskia River, the Mississippi River, the Missouri River, the Blackwater River, Mill Creek, the Chapman River, the Solomon River, the Saline River, the South Fork of Sappa Creek, Beaver Creek, Landsman Creek, Spring Creek, the South Fork of the Republican River, Bijou Creek, Comanche Creek, Wolf Creek, the Sybille River, Rock Creek, the Medicine Bow River, the North Platte River, the Green River, the Blacks Fork River, the Bear River, the Great Salt Lake, the Humbolt River, and finally the Truckee River, we eventually made our way into Tahoe.

A week later, I found myself barefoot on a sailboat, drifting across the lake, and staring out at snowcapped mountains. The wind had died, to our disappointment, and we were milling about the boat, simply admiring Tahoe's beauty.

"Check out the snow," said Hunter, staring out over the lake at the mountains. "It's June. Two weeks ago we could've been skiing."

"I heard you can still ski Mammoth," I added.

"Want to go next weekend?" Beights yelled from the tip of the boat. He was sitting with his legs hanging off the side, feet dipped into the water. Beights looked the perfect part for Tahoe. His hair was pulled back into a ponytail.

"We got to find jobs," said Ben.

"Yeah, or we could go skiing instead!" replied Beights with a laugh, mesmerized by the idea.

"Not sure how *you're* going to pay for it," said Ben, "But I got to find a job."

"Yeah, well, I'm getting a job outside," said Beights, as he came back to reality. "I'm not going to be stuck indoors. Not in this place."

"Look at the water," said Ben. "Blue as the ocean."

"You see the edge of the lake?" I asked. "Looks like the Caribbean."

"This place is pretty damn sweet," said Skip with a laugh. Skip tends to stick to the basics. All Skip has to do is say a few words, and laugh, and you know exactly what he's been thinking for hours. He has one of the world's greatest laughs.

"Your pictures didn't do it justice," Hunter said to Ben.

"We need some wind," said Ben. "Not bad lounging around, but I want to see this baby in action." That statement seemed to do the trick with the wind gods. Suddenly, hearing a loud shake in the sail and feeling a burst of air on my cheek, I knew that there was still some sailing to do.

"There we go, boys!" yelled Skip.

"That's what I'm talking about!" said Ben.

As the wind ripped across the lake, our fluttering sail shook full. With the wind came the sun, and with the sun came the light. When the sun shines, the world takes a deeper breath. When the sun shines in Tahoe, life pauses. Well, it's not life itself that pauses; in fact, it gets going with much more speed. The rest of us just stop and finally pay attention.

It was in that moment that the reality caught up with me. That was the moment that mattered. Only months before, our plans had been empty. Tahoe had been only a place of pictures and tales. Yet now these pictures were ours. All it took was a thought. The idea hatched at the bottom of a stream and grew as it adapted to life. It struggled to swim at first, but the struggle quickly faded. This idea was now afloat. This thought in the wind had reached our sail.

"Why don't we live in Tahoe?" we asked one day, sitting on the porch in Charlottesville.

Do you know how to make that happen? It's not as difficult as it may seem. You say: "Okay, let's do it." Of course, you have to mean it. When someone says, "Why don't we live in Tahoe?" you don't respond, "That sounds hard to figure out." Instead, you ask questions. "Where on the lake shall we live? How much are we willing to pay? Who should we call?"

I've always found that it has worked better for me if I think through questions as they arise, as opposed to sticking to preconceived notions. It seems simplistic, albeit extremely difficult in practice. But if I had written off the idea of living in Montana, Europe, and Tahoe from the start, this would be a vastly boring book. So I'm going to keep an open mind about things as much as possible. It seems to be serving me well so far.

I tried to warn everyone that we were coming. If you were a bar in Tahoe, or a music venue in San Francisco, you likely received advance notice of our arrival by a horrific attempt on my part at mass mail and CD promotion.

No calls. Not one. It appears we weren't the only band that had dreams of the Sierra Blue. And other bands were actually *bands*. They had their own songs and stuff (we were mainly a cover band playing old Rolling Stones, Grateful Dead, and Allman Brothers tunes). They had managers and equipment and vans and buses and people who wanted to hear them play. And *they* couldn't get gigs. Do you know how many times we performed that summer? Once. *Once!* No weekly gigs, no sold-out shows in San Fran, no groupies, no sex, drugs, and rock 'n' roll. Nope ... only one gig. But once was about all that we needed.

I've played music in a bar in Lake Tahoe. That's a great sentence too, isn't it? The great thing about it—well, there were a couple of great things about it, but one of them was the fact that people were there. Another is the fact that these people listened and they clapped and they cheered and they told us we were good. The last thing I'll mention is the fact that we were in Lake Tahoe, and we were a band, and we played music in the band, and we played music in Lake Tahoe in the band. Think about what everyone else was doing. To me, that was worth the drive.

So, *musical performance* was not the phrase of the summer. Yet that's not to say that music itself wasn't. As with all of my days, music was there. As with all of my days, the music was what I looked forward to. And we had music. And we played music. If we couldn't play for bars, we just said to hell with it, and watched movies all day, right? Hell, no. We played for ourselves. Sometimes that's the most rewarding, you know. In our lives, the intricacies are what we live for. The beautiful thing about music is that the intricacies never leave. They're there at a performance. They're there at a practice. They're there when you're with people. They're there when you're alone. Sometimes the intricacies are most alive when you're alone.

"Try to hold the E," Ben said to Beights, one evening as we were practicing around the cabin. "You know, just punch it like E ... E ... E ... E ... E ... E."

"Yeah," said Hunter, "and Hudson, let the organ ring over it. Add a little sustain."

"I'll come in after the break," said Ben, "with some light percussion."

"Hunter," I started to say, but then paused, "Just keep doing what you're doing." Hunter can play slide guitar better than anyone I know—he sounds like Derek Trucks.

With that, Skip ran into the house and slammed the door. He was out of breath, and it took him a second to speak.

"There's a damn bear in the backyard," he laughed.

"Where?" asked Ben.

"Arnie and I were playing horseshoes," he laughed again, "and he just walked out of the woods."

"I saw him yesterday," said Beights, trying to act like it was no big deal. "He's pretty harmless."

After turning from the window, eager to sneak a peak, Ben sat back down at the drums. "Didn't someone write a song about a bear?" Ben asked.

"Yeah," said Hunter, "think it was called 'Bear's Gone Fishing.'"

"Not this bear," Skip said with a grin. "This bear gone walking."

"Love that song," said Beights.

"You love *every* song," said Ben.

"Whatever, dude," Beights replied. "Just the good stuff."

"How do you define *good stuff?*" asked Ben.

"Can't define it," said Beights. "You can hear it, though."

"It's not the notes," I said. "Anyone can write the notes."

"What do you think it is?" asked Ben.

"I think it's the emotions in the songs," said Hunter.

"Yeah," said Beights. "Like 'Second that emotion' …"

"No," I replied, "It's not the emotions in the songs … it's the emotions in the musicians."

Do you want to know what I did every day? This might piss you off. It pisses *me* off that I'm not still doing it. We'll start with the night.

Coyotes howled in the night. Often, I would wake to their call. Think about this for a second. We're living in pretty modern times, don't you think? (Well, I guess everyone who's ever been alive has thought that.) But coyotes seem like a thing of the past, right? You can't really sleep to the sound of coyotes anymore—can you? That depends on where you sleep. For some reason, I got a great deal of pleasure from them. Somehow, I found symbolism in their echoing voices.

Every time I woke to the sound, it startled me. Every time it startled me, it forced me to think about where I was. Every time I thought about what I was doing, I thought about what everyone else was doing. And every time I thought about what everyone else was doing, I thought about what I was hypothetically *supposed* to be doing myself.

I was supposed to be in New York. I was supposed to be awake. I was supposed to be at a computer. I was supposed to be an investment banker. If you don't work for an investment bank in New York at some point in your life, you are equivalent to a piece of shit. You are a nothing. You will go nowhere. At least, that's what my schooling seemed to be telling me. And people didn't even *tell* me that! Some people even told me that I didn't have to be an investment banker. Those people were lying. Those people told me that out of dishonesty. They didn't mean it. They couldn't *possibly* have meant it. The people who told me I didn't have to be an investment banker only wished me harm. At least, this is what I told myself. But that was bullshit, and I knew it. I knew it all along.

Each time I heard a howl in the night, I didn't think about the West; I thought about New York. I thought about how glad I was *not* to be there, how sorry I felt for those who were there, and how good it felt to do what I actually wanted. (As an aside, I now live and work in Manhattan. How's that for irony? I love New York. I'll be here for a while.)

So that's what happened every night at about 3:00 AM. I would wake to the howling, think these thoughts, take a piss, pretend that the toilet was Goldman Sachs, and then go back to sleep feeling great about myself. What a way to sleep.

When I woke in the morning, it was sunny. It's always sunny in Tahoe, seriously. I think there are something like 320 days of sunshine a year there. On the other forty-five it only rains for about an hour. I actually saw it *snow* in Tahoe before I saw it rain. This was summer. I don't even distinctly remember seeing rain, but I think it may have rained one day. Maybe two, but I doubt if it was many more. When I woke up in the morning it was normally sunny.

I would then do something quite odd. I would put on long pants, a short-sleeved polo shirt, and loafers. What, was I going to a wedding? A funeral? Was I meeting George Bush or something? What the hell was I so dressed up for? Those are the looks I got from just about everybody. I did not look right at all. Not for Tahoe. Did you know that before my visit I called my boss and I asked him if I needed to bring suits? *Suits!* He couldn't believe I had asked him that. I'm sure I was almost fired for the question, but he let me show up eventually. If I wore a bathing suit and a Bob Marley T-shirt, I would be much more appropriately dressed than if I showed up in a damn suit. Tahoe is such a cool place to work; not that much work gets done in Tahoe. You might as well be in Italy.

Okay, this is the cool part. This part is supposed to be terrible, but I loved it. Driving to work was, in a word, awesome. Can you believe I just said that? I'll say it again. Driving to work was awesome. Do you know what I got to do? Naturally, I would toss in some Jerry Garcia or some bluegrass or some reggae or something that was just plain good. And then I would roll down the windows to let the sun in a little. Next came the air-conditioning. I'm talking tons of air-conditioning. Air-conditioning was key, because I was in long pants and that made zero sense to anybody. Wearing long pants made about as much sense as air-conditioning with the windows down, but I did it anyway.

At that point I felt like a damned million bucks. You're not supposed to feel that way on the way to work. Well you *are*, but not in the real world. And, I was excited. I would drive past all the cabins on our street and contemplate our neighborhood as I headed down toward the lake. I would spend the next half hour winding around its banks, driving on one of the most scenic roads in the United States, California State Highway 89. From Homewood to South Lake Tahoe, the only stoplight was the lake's occasional blinding reflection of the sun, which forced you to squint and slow down, yet only for a second. The rest of the time you were cruising along, passing entrances to state parks, passing under Sierra pines, passing by views of mountains, passing by waterfalls, passing the time as you would on vacation (not that I wasn't on vacation). Do you realize that I got to drive by Emerald Bay on the way *to work*?

Emerald Bay is apparently one of the world's most picturesque places. The bay is a cove on the southwestern part of Lake Tahoe.

Doesn't it just sound like a place you want to drive by? Emerald Bay. Doesn't the yellow brick road end there? More pictures are taken in a year of the bay than just about anywhere.

Emerald Bay is to Tahoe as the Mediterranean is to the Atlantic: if you were in a plane it would have a similar look to it. At the crest of the bay, the eye of Tahoe seems to squint into the sun to allow water to rush into its cove. This water is always a color of the deepest blue. And in the center of the bay is an island, a small island fit for little more than admiring. Each morning I would drive around the bay, the bay being my morning "traffic," if you will, and each morning it was heart lifting. Each morning, I would glare out into the bay at its deepest point, past the island, past the sailboats, into the eye of Tahoe, and beyond into the mountains. And as I rounded further, I would follow the road up onto a tall ridge, a tall ridge only as wide as the road itself, and I would reach the best drivable view I've ever seen. Far down to the left was the bay; far down to the right, Cascade Lake (a second lake fed by waterfall); straight ahead, Lake Tahoe; and in the distance, well, everything that the word distance brings to mind, if you know what I mean. At that point I had ten minutes until my morning drive was over. Emerald Bay was my clock. Tahoe is such a splendid keeper of the time.

18
A Day in the Life

Above anything, the broker who I worked for taught me one key lesson: never be a stockbroker. I learned that daily.

"Paul, why do you want to do this? You should never do this," he often said.

His primary goal for my summer's education was to convince me solidly that I never wanted his job.

"Have I convinced you not to do this yet? I hope so," he might say.

Or, "You're still showing up here? Dammit, what am I doing wrong?"

What I didn't tell him was that he didn't need to do any preaching. I knew the first minute I introduced myself that there was no way in hell I was going to be a stockbroker. In fact, I knew that before I even called him for the job. What I did not tell him was that working in his office achieved two essential goals of mine: first, his firm had the name "financial" in it, which was pretty much all I demanded for my resume at the time. Second, his firm was based in Lake Tahoe, and that suited me just fine. From there, I figured any unexpected learning that took place was simply an added benefit.

My job primarily entailed sitting in my boss's office. When he was on the phone, I read. When he was off the phone, we talked. We talked about brokerage, technology, hedge funds, Greenspan, corruption, purity, you name it. We bonded primarily over the idea that there was much more to life than spending it inside all day. That's why he lived in Tahoe. That's why *I* lived in Tahoe. That bond held us together from 10:00 AM to 4:30 PM every Monday through Wednesday, my workweek. It was stressful, to say the least.

"Market's gone crazy," he said to me one day.

"What's up?" I asked.

"Everything," he said. "Everything is up. Yesterday, everything was down."

"What's going on?" I asked.

"People are just crazy, that's all," he responded.

"Jobs report was strong today," I said.

"Yeah, that's why it's up," he said. "Everyone's just focused on that one damn number. Yesterday, earnings looked bad, and the market was in the shitter."

"People focus too much on the short term," he added.

"The problem," I said, "is that everyone focuses on the same market."

"What do you mean?" he asked.

"Everyone in the world is focused on the stock market," I said. "Hard to make a killing when everyone's paying attention."

"Yeah," he replied. "The way to do it isn't to trade the stocks. The way to do it is to start the company that people trade."

"The trick isn't even creating a new company," I said. "The trick is creating a new market no one has ever even seen before. Look at Bill Gates—he started a new market entirely."

After a few moments of staring at the painting on the wall, apparently deep in thought, he looked over at me, and said, "You know the best example I've seen?"

"What?" I asked.

"Art," he replied.

"Yeah," I responded, knowing exactly what he meant. "Creative arbitrage."

These are the kinds of things we would talk about during my intense workdays, which ended at 4:30 PM, I'll remind you, from Monday to Wednesday. I'll remind you again.

Now, the afternoons are what I'm talking about. Whether it was a sail out into the middle of the lake with my boss and a six pack of Pacificos, or sitting on the beach with a book, you couldn't beat the afternoons. I primarily read Bill Bryson, as I thought he had the coolest job in the world—traveling to distant corners of the planet and then coming home to write about it.

Did I mention there were beaches in Tahoe? Did I specifically tell you that there are beaches 6,225 feet above the sea? Well, there are. And there are seventy-five miles of shoreline, plenty enough to find a nice spot to settle down for a beer and a book or what have you.

Let's go ahead and get this out of the way: Lake Tahoe is quite a large lake (twenty-three miles long and thirteen miles wide, with a surface area of 195 square miles). Two-thirds of the lake is in California. One-third is in Nevada. Lake Tahoe is the second-deepest lake in the world, with a maximum depth of 1,645 feet (Lake Titicaca, in Peru, holds first place). The deepest part of the lake is ninety-two feet *below* the level of Carson City, which lies in the valley east of Tahoe.

As a quick anecdote, some drunkards calculated the depth of Tahoe as accurately as the U.S. government. On July 4, 1875, two dudes used a leaded champagne bottle and fishing line to peruse the lake in order to find the deepest point. Their drunken precision was immaculate: 1,645 feet. The U.S. Coast and Geodetic Survey of 1922 revealed the same thing. They were probably just as drunk, though.

Happy yet? Not me—you still don't understand how big this thing is. The lake is as long as the English Channel is wide, and its width is half that of the San Francisco Bay. To give you a hint, Lake Tahoe holds enough water to cover the state of Texas to a depth of 8 1/2 inches. Eight and a half inches! It can cover California with 14 inches. Take Lake Mead, for example. Lake Mead is backed up 227 miles into the Grand Canyon by the Hoover Dam. Lake Mead is considered one of the largest man-made lakes in the world. Tahoe contains nearly four times the maximum capacity of Lake Mead. That's a lot of water. The Panama Canal averages 700 feet in width and 50 feet in depth, and such a canal could be filled by Tahoe's water and extended completely around the earth, at the equator, with enough water remaining to fill another channel from San Francisco to New York. Lake Tahoe is quite the large lake.

The best dock on Tahoe is by far McKinney's old joint. You could dock your boat elsewhere. But then again, you couldn't dock it and then step three feet into the bar and order a cold one. Well you could, but you wouldn't still be standing on a dock. You'd be on dry ground.

In 1875, John Washington McKinney built one of the first boathouses on the lake. This boathouse doubled as a bar/clubhouse (it appears Mr. McKinney was one cool fellow). McKinney's was quite the popular spot, and for good reason. To quote my Tahoe history buff, Mr. E. B. Scott, "John Muir was a regular guest at McKinney's, and the famous California naturalist and outdoorsman aptly described the stately sugar pines surrounding the resort as 'priests of the forest extending their arms in benediction over the congregation.'" Why is it that we always seem to become a little more religious once the wine hits our veins? Perhaps that's why this bar still exists 129 years later—only now it's called Chamber's Lodge.

Well, lucky for me then—I could walk to Chamber's Lodge from our house in Homewood. In fact, I did, quite frequently. Chamber's beach was my favorite place to wind down after a long, hard day at the office. Talk about peaceful.

Tahoe bears not a single hectic spot, and Chamber's must have started the trend. Its tall wooden pier sits above the Sierra Blue as if it were a fence looking after a ranch. At the base of the pier lies the boathouse, a simple structure with a single-pitched roof, resembling a small old-fashioned schoolhouse sitting silently at the edge of a prairie. This place *is* Lake Tahoe. Of all Tahoe's homes and of all its views, no building is as pleasant and no view is as breathtaking as this one.

On my frequent afternoon visits, Chamber's beach became my home. At the beach I could settle down into my chair, run the sand across my toes, and peer out into the water at the arriving boats. I could admire the boaters as they carelessly walked the length of the pier until they disappeared into the bar. I could do all of this with beer and book in hand.

On certain days, the beach was too peaceful—serenity to the point of boredom. On those days, I often chose more for myself. My favorite secondary pastime was strolling, yet not on foot—on my bike. Somehow, gliding down calm streets watching the neighbors return to their nests gave me a similar sense of relaxation as watching the water. Some days I actually exerted physical energy on these strolls, enough energy that I will go as far as to label it *exercise*, although those days were few and far between. The energetic days took me to great places. The slow ones did as well. One of the best places was a little spot deep in the forest behind our neighboring town of Tahoma. Hidden Lake, it was called.

Hidden Lake became my secret garden. You see, it took some energy to get there. First you had to leave the sidewalk and bike down an old logging road until the road narrowed to a thin trail. Then you had to follow this trail through the pines, over difficult sections of rock and root, and up hills much longer than expected. But the garden was well worth any trek.

Upon arrival, I would park my bike against a nearby tree and meander down a short path until I had to swipe the vines away from my face to continue. As the vines began to rise, it quickly became apparent that I was about to enter a magical landscape. In the midst of the deep pine forest, I discovered a small, unexpected field of rich green grass and colorful wildflowers. Beside the field lay a still pond, a small pond covered in unusually large lily pads. In tandem, the field and the pond appeared perfect. Hidden Lake is not the spectacular sight that Tahoe is. This lake presents a more mindful view. I loved the thought that very few people were likely even to know the place.

Do you know how much water Hidden Lake can hold? Who cares; it isn't very much. Probably only about as much as your average swimming pool. That's not the point this time.

The one thing Hidden Lake lacked was trout.

If I wasn't sailing the lake, drinking a beer at Chamber's, biking to who-knows-where, playing my keyboard, or pining away for the perfect picture, I was deep in search of trout—that was for sure. I eventually decided to combine the last two activities. You quickly discover that where there are trout, there are pictures; the two are actually one and the same, if you think about it. And you know the sad thing? I can't really say that I ever found trout. Norman Maclean may be haunted by waters, but I must admit that with me, the water is not the problem. I can find the water, just not the trout. I am haunted by trout.

"Pull up!" yelled Hunter, as we fished a mountain pond one afternoon.

I yanked the rod into the air, but the fish was gone.

"Damn," said Hunter, "You missed him. You got to be quicker."

"How do you know when he takes the fly?" I asked.

"You'll see the fly disappear underwater for a split second," he said.

Of course, the fly, which I could barely even see in my hand, was now thirty yards away on the end of my line. If he thought I could see the damn thing in the water, he was sadly mistaken.

I can't count the number of days that I searched for trout without finding them. They were too many to recall. Trout appeared to dislike me. I can count the number of trout that I caught, though. That's easy. One. I lived in Lake Tahoe for an entire summer and caught one lousy trout. And it wasn't even the number that killed me, it was the size. The trout truly was lousy in size; probably ten to twelve inches. Now, that's not a bad trout, I know. But it wasn't a trout of stories. I needed a trout of stories for *this* story. I had envisioned this great evolutionary analogy, involving trout, that hinged on my landing a pig of a trout in Tahoe. You see, if I caught this trout, this story would be beautiful. Hidden symbolism could've been traced through these pages, just as trout grace the stream.

The analogy would begin with that initial summer, our Western expedition. You would think about Aspen and our first attempt at fly-fishing. You would remember Chas holding the fly above the trout, expecting the trout to rise, and you would laugh at our innocence. In a way it would symbolize our youth and begin to highlight the greater meaning of this tale. Then you would picture the Madison, and think of Montana, and remember that we did actually catch trout in Montana, albeit small ones. You would begin to feel that we had grown up in some manner, and at least recognize that we had the wherewithal to respect the water that we were fishing. You would see that young boys had grown up, but that they also had much to learn. Then your mind would wander further and settle upon Europe, where we weren't allowed to fish for trout. We were not of the local aristocracy. You would think of the disappointment that we faced daily at not being able to pursue our dreams as we envisioned them. You would begin to see how the tides of history taught us the painful lesson that what you seek, you may not find. You would empathize with our sorrow. But the kicker would come from Tahoe.

I was to tell the most glorious tale of catching the largest trout I'd ever seen, a never-ending rainbow, and you would, alas, discover our wisdom. Everything would make sense. This story would take on new meaning. This book would become a classic. Yet that didn't happen. This analogy was ruined, this symbolism lost.

But wait? Is it? This may be *better*. What would it mean if I caught a trophy trout in Tahoe—that I had grown into a man, and had stood the test of time, and had conquered nature to the point that catching trout was as easy as a cast into the stream? Perhaps, and that would be the wrong direction for the story to go, the wrong conclusion. The lesson would be that life is easy, that life is like a dream, a fairy tale. But this is *real*. So the ending must be real as well. If I had caught a never-ending rainbow, it would be like this book becoming an immediate best seller. It would be as if thinking of an idea would make it come to life in an instant. That is not true to life. It can happen, but it takes some time. This book can't be a best seller; that's just not the way things are going to go. But it can be beautiful, and it can be a start. Its lesson will *not* be that of instant glory, but instead, of steady progress and truth. The meaning will come from the fish that wasn't, not the fish that was. And that's the better story, and that's the truth, and that's what happened to me in Tahoe.

I caught one fish. This fish was not a fish of stories, but a fish of reality. As my fly floated downstream toward the still-fading rise in the water, I was casting at a goal then beyond me. Yet, as I went back to this goal, back to this rise, time and time again, something changed. Time was now on my side. My persistence prevailed. The fish that never was now appeared. He wasn't a large fish, a trophy fish, but he was a fish nonetheless, and a *trout*.

This trout now took my fly.

The moment was unspoken, yet contained words beyond imagination. What it told me was a story about myself. It was an unexpected ending to the analogy, yet the analogy was now more meaningful. I didn't need to catch a trophy. The brilliant thing about fly-fishing is that the lasting reward doesn't lie on a scale. You don't fish for the picture of the fish; you fish for the bite and for its cast. The same is true with writing. The same is true with this book. The beauty of this book will not be in its sales; it will not set records as the largest rainbow seen to man. But it will be a trout. And it will be a smaller trout, but someone will cast a fly toward it. This person, if only a single person in the world, just as I was the lone fisherman in the stream, will catch this trout, without anyone watching, but they will catch it. The catch, not the size, is what matters. This fisherman will leave the stream with a lesson, with a memory, that only he can describe to himself. This memory will be a part of him, and it will be with him the next time that he casts his line. This is the beauty of fishing, this is the beauty of writing, and this is my purpose, so I'm told. Not just writing, but creating. Creating something for someone to catch and hold on to. I can tie this fly in numerous ways. I just need enough time and enough thread to keep going.

The day that I caught my Tahoe fish truly was one of my most memorable. It was a day in which dreams were spoken of and discussed. I sat on the bank of the river with my fishing guide, Hunter, and we began to talk. This talk was not of fish or of streams, but larger talk—the talk about life and where we were going.

"You think you're going back to Atlanta next year?" Hunter asked, as we sat on the bank watching the water.

"I don't know, perhaps," I said. "May go to New York to do the finance thing."

"Sounds terrible," he replied.

"I'd rather come back out here," I remarked. "Rainer and I have talked about moving to Colorado at some point."

"Now, that would be cool," said Hunter. "Maybe you could get a job as a photographer on the slopes or something."

"Or I could play tunes in a bar," I added. "What about you?"

"I'd like to go to Jackson Hole again," he said. "I could probably get the same job I had last summer."

"Fly shop?" I asked.

"Yeah, I may even be able to guide some," he said.

"Now, that's what I'm talking about," I replied.

"But I'll probably end up settling for a real job," Hunter added.

"Wish we could just live out here forever," I said.

"I know," said Hunter. "Why is there so much pressure to sit in an office somewhere?"

After a few minutes of thought, I turned and asked Hunter a question.

"You know how whenever we travel out here, we seem to think of it as our long-lost home?"

"Yeah," he said. "Feels like home to me."

"Well, I wonder what people who live here think about us?"

"What do you mean?" he asked.

"I mean, we're invading their turf. They're the ones that live here."

"I don't know," he replied. "They probably get tired of us catching all of their damn fish, though!" he laughed.

It was a great afternoon. We spoke of where we were supposed to go, where we were likely to go, and compared it to where we actually wished we could go. We talked of dream jobs, of working for

National Geographic and the like, as photographers paid to travel the world. The talk was comforting and exciting and the kind of talk that you later learn to rely on. I broke down and mentioned this writing (against trusted advice to keep it personal). Hunter thought that this book was a great idea and he supported it. Yet I'm sure he thought it was nothing more than a dream. But at that point in our conversation, anything was possible. He began to dream my dream with me. He thought I could make this a story of everyone. I could tell each of our stories in parts and then tie them together with a profound net large enough to bring us all ashore. One chapter could be about me, the next about him, and so on. It was only natural for him to think that way; to each of us our own story is better. Yet deep down, I knew that this was going to be a story of my own.

The talk was cut short by the movement of the sun. As it sank behind the mountains, the valley began to darken, and the fish began to rise. Perhaps it's better that we moved on to the fishing—dreams can fade the more you think them through. I'm glad I haven't had the time to think through the dream of this book too much; I'm still asleep, and I am loving it.

What better time of day than dusk? I dream that dusk could last for hours. But if so, dusk's meaning would fade with the light. There is a reason that the sun sets more abruptly than we would hope. There is a reason why the light stays that way for just a few minutes. It is the brisk, yet eternal, flash in time that holds the moment true. It is within this quick, closing window that the world readjusts in unison. Aside from this cherished calm, there is no other time in which everyone's mood is the same.

19
Weekend Excursion

In general, what do you do with a weekend? Do you stay and enjoy your home at a relaxed pace? Do you pack up the car and head to a new place? Once again, not everyone is of the traveling disposition, but I suggest both. You can't appreciate the one without the other. When you're relishing the comforts of home, have lunch outside, and talk about places you may want to visit. When you visit those places while on vacation, try not to talk too much about home. Sometimes it's best to let the new scenery guide your conversations to places they never would've gone. There's nothing like a foreign view to bring forth abstract thoughts that otherwise would remain hidden.

So we spent our weekends two ways in Tahoe: both there and gone. If you don't mind, let me focus on the *gone* for a bit. You should have a taste of *there* already.

My first gone involved a plane. A big plane. A jet. A commercial jet. I was getting out of there. Not because I wanted to leave, but because of music. There was a certain event that I needed to see. I needed to see it badly. It was far from a deterrent that this music took place in the hills of Tennessee. I was flying to attend the first annual Bonnaroo Music Festival. (*Oh great*, you say, *you are a damn hippie, aren't you?*) Possibly, but to me it's different. I like music. I like to listen to music. I like to play music. I like to watch music. Music just makes sense to me. Bonnaroo was merely an excuse to be around even more music than usual. I guess that wasn't a very good job of convincing you I'm not a hippie, was it?

Now, I thought about walking you through the fields of endless tents to the various stages and giving you a *Rolling Stone*–type synopsis of the event. I thought I might mention that this was the Woodstock of our generation, and talk about the heat, the rain, youth, rebellion, etc. I thought I might review each band and its performance. I thought I might talk about the *jamband* counterculture and get into the depths of why so many people avoid the radio. I thought I might talk about a movement. I was going to take you on a little musical journey, and you were going to meet all of the people I walked beside along the way. I was somewhat of a wanderer in Tennessee. I thought you might want to wander with me. As I thought longer, however, my desire to move forward in that direction faded with each step. I decided that my thoughts on the music were better kept to myself. My time at Bonnaroo was better spent as *my* time. No need to drag you into something you don't want to read. Besides, it would largely be a self-serving endeavor.

The most story-worthy part of my trip to Bonnaroo was not the music, but my ticket. My ticket had a great story. It went on a little trip. In fact, my ticket's trip is still going. You see, my ticket never made it to the event. From the printing press, the ticket went to my house in Atlanta. The ticket then hopped on a plane with my parents to Reno and took a short drive up the road into Tahoe. For a few days, my ticket sat on the desk of a hotel in Squaw Valley, simply admiring the view. From here, the ticket's story takes a turn for the worse. Instead of ending up in my pocket, it was accidentally left behind on the desk at the hotel. It needed my pocket. It craved my pocket. But the ticket sat lonely on the desk, as my parents checked out and left it behind forever.

Hours later, I remembered the ticket. Hours later, I drove to the hotel. My visions of the ticket sitting nicely on the desk were shattered by the sight of cleanliness. I asked the front desk clerk where my ticket could've gone. After careful consideration of the facts presented to me, I deciphered that the ticket had left its spot on the desk. It took a tumbling fall into the trash can. It then took a ride down the hall and into the elevator. My ticket got out at the basement and strolled out the door. By this point, the ticket must have been scared to death. It may have been crying. It was definitely crying when it gazed up at the large and eminent green trash compactor.

At the point of my arrival, it was almost a mathematical certainty that my ticket was sitting somewhere in the trash compactor—where, I was not quite sure. I demanded to see the scene of the crime. I began asking questions.

"So you think it's in there?" I asked.

"I think so. I don't know where else it would be."

"What about a Lost and Found?"

"Sir, we've checked."

"What about the front desk?"

"Sir, I'm afraid it was thrown away."

"And you think it's in there?"

"I'm pretty sure."

"Have they emptied this today?"

"No, they come in the morning."

"I think I'm going to look inside."

"Sir?"

"I think I'm going in."

"Pardon me, sir, but why don't you just buy another ticket?"

"You don't understand. It's sold out."

"Why don't you go another time?"

"There is no other time. Besides, I already have a flight. I think I'm going in."

"Sir, this is a trash *compactor*. It crushes the trash. There's no telling where the ticket is. And it's dangerous to climb in there."

"That's a risk I'm going to have to take," I said. "I'll just look in the first few bags."

And I did. I climbed in the damn thing and took a look around. Picture me at ten o'clock at night behind a hotel in Squaw Valley, with a flashlight, climbing into a large green container of trash bags.

That was me. I wanted to find that ticket. The people at the hotel thought I was a raving lunatic.

I never found the ticket. It is sitting somewhere in a California landfill, hopefully on top of the pile, with a nice view. I ended up having to pay double for a new one. I didn't really care though. Bonnaroo was my Woodstock. Did you think I was going to miss out on Woodstock? If you did, you're insane!

I drove to San Francisco the first weekend I got the chance. It's somewhat of an odd feeling driving your car across the Golden Gate Bridge. Once you cross the bridge, you want to stop. You want to turn around and drive across again. With images of the Golden Gate burnt deeply into my brain, it didn't make much sense that I would just cross the bridge once and then move on. Strangely, you have to.

There I stood with a cigarette. I hate cigarettes. It wasn't that I liked them *then*, but hate them *now*. I hated them then, too. I never smoke. But, for some reason, it just felt like the right time to step outside and smoke a cigarette. First of all, she was going to have one. I thought it would be nice to have one with her. I can't remember her name. If you ever want a cigarette, you should track her down. We had met the previous day in Tahoe. She drove to San Francisco with us. She was the friend-of-a-friend type of girl. She was on a trip across the country with her boyfriend. During the middle of the trip, they decided they didn't like each other. They stopped dating. They had three more weeks in the trip to go. Awkward. I met this girl when they drove through Tahoe. Somehow, the fact that we had only just met called for a cigarette. We needed to get to know each other. But that was only part of it. I was having one of those larger moments. I knew the cigarette would only aid in the moment. I took a drag. I then blew the smoke into the damp, dark San Francisco air. I felt alive.

"So, you're in a band?" she asked.

"Yeah," I said. "We all moved out here for the summer."

"What do you play?"

"Guitar and piano."

"Can you sing?"

"You wouldn't want to hear it," I laughed. "Only sounds good in the shower."

"I wish I could play piano," she said.

"I'll teach you sometime." (I was doing my best to hit on her.)

"So, I guess music is your thing," she said. "Do you want to do it full-time?"

"I guess that's the dream," I said. "But I'm not counting on it. What do you want to do?"

"Travel around," she said. "Not really looking to get serious about anything just yet." It was my kind of answer. It was my kind of night.

Let's figure out what was so great about that cigarette. It is important to take a step back, to explain the chain of events that led up to the cigarette, in order to get a better feel for it.

The afternoon began when we left the cabin in Homewood, at about 3:00 PM, and drove at a leisurely pace toward San Francisco. The sun beamed down the entire drive. Our conversations were equally bright. Upon arrival, in order to fuel up, I had a classic pastrami sandwich on sourdough bread from a tiny little shop on the corner. We then walked up an unusually slanted hill, typical for San Francisco, to the door of a friend's apartment. The cigarette girl and her ex-boyfriend had a friend from home with whom we planned to stay.

I had no idea whom we were about to meet. The door opened. What are the odds? An Atlanta guy opened the door—someone I knew. I knew about five people who happened to be living in the city of San Francisco at the time. Two of them lived in the same apartment—the same apartment with the friend of my new acquaintances, the friend we were going to stay with. I had no intention of running into these people. Small world, isn't it? After a beer or two on their balcony, we hopped in a cab to head out for the evening. Minutes later, we were standing across the street from the Fillmore West. Vida

Blue was playing at the Fillmore. Sold out. Damn. So we walked across the street and into another show.

Topaz was scheduled to play in about an hour. The opening band was on stage warming up the crowd. The band was centered around a lead oboe player. Think about that for a second. *Lead oboe*—in a rock 'n' roll band? The guy could rip it, too. That deserved a cigarette in itself. But I needed a cigarette for other reasons. I needed to step outside. It was the night of my first trip to San Francisco. I'd always wanted to see San Francisco. It was a night of music and a night with new people. It was a new night in itself. It was a night that I was off on my own doing exactly what I wished to be doing. Somehow, the new city, the new people, the new music, the new night—all of it just called for a cigarette. Now I hate cigarettes, and I never smoke them, but that was a damn good one. I'm quite glad I had it. Cigarettes are awful.

My friends from Tahoe left the next morning, but I stayed on. This was my first visit to the streets of San Francisco. I was in no rush to leave them. Besides, my cousin lived there. She had a guest bedroom that I intended to put to good use.

After dropping off my bag and taking a quick shower, I hit the morning streets. For some reason, San Francisco is the city least set up for walking, but one of the best cities to walk around. Possibly it's because San Francisco is like Europe, in that many places are more accessible by foot. Driving in San Francisco doesn't always make the most sense. So, you hoof it. You walk up streets, down avenues, up hills, down town—importantly, you walk.

Each corner presented distinctive panoramas. Everything seemed so odd to me—blatantly different from what I was used to. The smell of the ocean miraculously blended with an urban scent. One minute, a brisk wind brushed past as I stepped into a humid cloud. In that moment, the streets were empty, except for a few people rushing by at a hurried pace. The next thing I knew, the sun was shining down, and the entire city was on a pleasant afternoon jog. To be honest, I didn't quite understand it. I need to go back to reevaluate.

I threw out this comment in a conversation once to gauge the reaction: "San Francisco is the most European American city." Not many agreed. I agreed, but I guess I had to. Of course, since then I've been to New Orleans and moved to New York.

It was kind of nice walking around alone; everything was on my schedule. My first stop after brunch was the tram. You've got to love cities with trams. I trammed it to the pier. The pier was nice for a tourist spot. Great crab. But it was too crowded for my intentions. I guess my intentions were none other than to see as much as possible.

As requested, the taxi let me out on Haight Street. Talk about a street. I'm not sure how I felt about walking down Haight alone. I did it anyway, although with slight unease. Haight Street is much more run-down than I would have thought: dirty, empty, and dark. But I needed to be there. I needed to see Haight and Ashbury. How could I call myself a music fan without ever seeing Haight and Ashbury?

On the four corners of Haight and Ashbury I envisioned a classic record store, a guitar store, a bustling café, and possibly God standing on the sidewalk. What did I find? Typical—a damn Starbucks and a damn Gap! This pissed me off greatly. Normally, I don't even get pissed off. I stayed for about twenty seconds, long enough to walk through the intersection and keep on going. Typical!

I was now looking for a destination—Amoeba Records. On my way down Haight toward Amoeba, I saw a sign for an Irish pub. It was 4:00 PM. *That would probably be a great spot for a beer in a few hours*, I thought. When I walked past the door, I did a double take. Noise, and a lot of it. I took a step back. The pub was packed. Not a barstool empty. It was 4:00 PM. I walked inside. Everyone in the Irish pub was Irish, accents and all. How European. Where else in America do you walk into an Irish pub and find it full of Irish drinkers? That's the goal—it just doesn't happen often. I stood at the back and simply took it all in.

"What'll it be?" said the bartender.

I had no intention of drinking that afternoon, but what the hell?

"I'll have a Guinness," I said. Seemed fitting.

That was a great Guinness—one of my all-time greatest, simply for the fact that while I drank the lager, Irish voices filled the air. Loud Irish voices. Drunk Irish voices. Happy, drunk Irish voices. That's the way to drink Guinness—around happy, drunk Irish voices.

My stomach felt a little full after the Guinness. Getting back to my walk down Haight Street was the perfect activity.

When I entered Amoeba Records, I felt like I was walking into a long-lost home. The people just looked right. The place just felt right.

"Can I help you?" someone asked, as I was aimlessly wandering.

"Yeah," I said. "I'm looking for an old Jerry Garcia Band album." He laughed to himself, but then quickly tried to cover it up. Apparently I was not the first person to ask for a Jerry Garcia album on Haight Street.

The Jerry Garcia section of the music bin was about three feet wide. In other places it would contain about ten albums in total. Like I said, I felt at home. Amoeba Records is the best record store in America. It's the kind of record store that sorts out all of the crap and only carries the good stuff, and lots of it.

20
Desolation Wilderness

"What a day," said Beights, as we hiked up the trail.

"Not bad," said Hunter, hiking right behind him.

"It's nice out," I confirmed. It was a gorgeous day, cool and crisp for a summer afternoon. Hunter, Beights, and I had been planning the camping trip since the day we arrived in Tahoe. We were walking on a trail heading deep into the Desolation Wilderness, the national forest bordering the eastern side of the lake. With a name like that, we were eager to explore.

"How far do ya'll want to go?" I asked.

"Legs are feeling good," said Hunter. "Let's cover some ground."

The plan was to hike about ten miles. Considering the elevation changes, we had a full day ahead.

We stopped for lunch at an elevation break, where the forest opened up to a magnificent view. Miles and miles below, Lake Tahoe was shimmering in the sun.

As I stared out at the lake, two hikers appeared in the distance, heading in our direction. As they approached, they stopped for a sip of water. The two guys appeared to be in their late thirties.

"Howdy," I said.

"Afternoon," said the taller one, as he pulled out his water bottle.

"Whew," said the other, throwing his pack against a tree. "Mind if we stop for a rest?"

"Not at all," said Beights. "Make yourself at home."

"Quite the view," said the tall one.

"Not bad," I said. "Good spot for a break."

"You guys from around here?" asked the shorter one, as he searched for a place to sit down.

"No," said Hunter. "We're from Virginia."

"But we're out here for the summer," said Beights. "We live down the way in Homewood."

"Nice town," said the tall one.

"How about you?" I asked.

"We're from the valley," said the shorter one.

"Silicon Valley," clarified the tall one. "Up here on vacation."

"How long you out here for?" Hunter asked.

"Out here?" said the short one, as he looked out into the distance. "Just a few days. But we've got a lot planned after this."

"Sounds like a good vacation," said Hunter.

"Actually," laughed the tall one, "we've got time on our side. We're in venture capital—we were both laid off after the tech bubble."

"We're taking the time to travel around," said the short one. "Making the best of it."

"Not bad," said Hunter.

"Not for now," said the tall one. "We'll have to get another job at some point."

"How old are you guys?" asked the short one.

"Twenty-one," said Hunter. "About to start our last year of college."

"Damn," said the tall one. "That's such a great age. You guys are doing the right thing, being out here."

"Enjoy it," said the short one. "Before you know it, things will fly away from you."

"We are," said Beights. "Don't worry."

"You think you're in a rush," said the tall one, "but you've got more time than you think. Just keep that in mind."

"We will," said Hunter. "Thanks."

"Well," said the tall one, "we better get back on the trail."

"Enjoy the afternoon," I said.

"Good talking to you," said the short one.

"You too," said Beights.

"Have a good one," said Hunter.

They picked up their backpacks, took one last sip of water, and continued onward.

"Being laid off doesn't seem so bad," Beights said to Hunter and me.

"Not when you live in Cali," said Hunter.

"That Internet thing sure messed up a lot of jobs," I said.

"I know," said Hunter. "Everyone out here's out of a job."

"The tech bubble was like a damn revolution," said Beights.

"Think we'll read about it one day?" asked Hunter. "Like, in the history books? The Industrial Revolution … The Tech Revolution … I wonder what's next?"

"We need another Renaissance," I said. "I bet that was cool to live through."

"Yeah," said Beights. "All the talk these days is money, money, money. We need a *creative* revolution."

"Think how cool that would be," I said. "All the talk would be music … film … art."

After giving it some thought, I added, "Wouldn't it be cool if everyone was *required* to take a year off after college to do something creative?"

"Like what?" asked Hunter.

"I don't know," I said. "Like make a film, write a book, record music, just anything out of the ordinary."

"Now you're talking," said Beights.

"I like it," said Hunter. "Like, if you couldn't get a job until you'd completed some creative venture of some sort."

"It would force people to figure out what they like," I said. "Too many people figure that out way too late, it seems."

"A year's a lot of time though," said Hunter. "Takes money to take a year off."

"I know," I replied. "Maybe we could create some kind of foundation or something to help fund it."

"It'd be cool to see what your friends ended up making," said Beights.

"It'd at least give us a lot more to talk about," I said. "Talking about jobs gets old. And if people were forced to do something creative, I think it would inspire a lot of people to stick with it."

"But some people aren't that creative," said Beights. "Most people are pretty happy taking normal jobs."

"I know," I said. "I guess you can't force creativity. But we could at least force everyone to take a year off. I bet people would do some pretty cool things with the time."

"Like the Australians," said Hunter. "They've got it figured out. It seems everyone in Australia takes a year off to travel at some point."

"Yeah," said Beights. "They're everywhere. All seem to love it, too."

"I'm taking a year off for sure at some point," I said.

"Hell, yeah," said Hunter. "Can't wait."

After another minute or two, it seemed time to move on.

"Ya'll want to move up the trail?" asked Beights.

"Yeah, I guess," I replied. "Let's do it."

We headed up the trail, continuing to dream out loud the entire afternoon. By the time we went to bed, we were going to cure the world. All the world needed was a creative jolt. We planned to give it to them.

21

Highway 1

Why is it that the last of anything that we do always stands out as the most memorable? The last night, the last weekend, the last trip—why is this our first thought? Why write off earlier experience simply because it took place earlier? To this I do not know the answer.

It was my last weekend in California, the weekend I remember most.

The last note of the concert hung in the air longer than it should have. It was supposed to fade away into the bay, but it lingered. I think the note wanted to stick around for a while and admire the view. The setting was, in a word, spectacular!

The Greek Theatre was quite the musical venue. The outdoor amphitheater mimicked Red Rocks in more ways than one. The stage rested high upon a hill in Berkley, which was an ingenious place to rest. The Greek Theatre was perched above the campus of U. C. Berkley, with a mighty view of the San Francisco Bay. We drove down from Tahoe to see a band. More importantly, we drove down from Tahoe to see music in the Greek Theatre. We drove down from Tahoe to explore new territory. This was our final excursion of the summer. The next Saturday I was set to depart on the long drive home, after a brief stop in Los Angeles.

"Hudson?" someone said, as I walked by with a beer, on the way to our seats.

I turned around and saw my buddy from Innsbruck, Wes Harden.

"Dude, what are you doing here?" he asked with a laugh.

"Whoa," I said. "Chancellor! What's the word?" I did not expect to see Chet in San Francisco. He was living in Atlanta at the time.

"We're out here visiting some folks," he said. "Do you live here?"

"No," I responded. "I'm in Tahoe for the summer. Drove down with some friends for the show."

"Nice," Wes replied, "I've seen more random people here; it's amazing."

"I know," I said. "Everyone seems to be on the same page."

"Hey," said Wes. "We're headed back into the city later for an after-party. Ya'll want to come with?"

"I would," I said, "but we're taking off after the show. Headed up to the Redwoods."

"You're always one step ahead, aren't you?" Wes said with a laugh, as he took a drag of his cigarette.

"No," I said. "Always one step behind."

As the music echoed through the night, the lights of San Francisco brightened up the sky, with chilly wet water in between. Surreal is a good word, so I think I'll use that. The night was surreal.

Most people were headed into San Francisco for the after-party. We were headed north. It was 11:00 PM on Friday night. Sounds like a good time to begin the bulk of a road trip, doesn't it? Why not? What were we going to do, sleep our last weekend away?

As the others turned left toward drinks and beds, we veered away and headed up the road into the night. The goal was Highway 1, the infamous drive up the California coast. You have the option of taking Highway 1 immediately, but we needed to cover some ground. It's a long way to the Redwoods. We didn't have a whole lot of time on our hands.

I had the plan. The perfect route was essential. Luckily for me, I knew it—at least, it looked good on a map. According to paper, you can take 101, the expressway, to the town of Cloverdale. There the road intersects with Highway 128, which is a direct shot to the coast. I told the group that we'd be in a Holiday Inn by 12:30 AM, with an ocean view in the morning. That sounded good to me.

My plan failed miserably. To start, Highway 128 is a two-lane road. This two-lane road may be the curviest road I've ever driven on. It is dead straight on the map. This winding road allows a maximum speed of roughly 20 mph. Driving 20 mph on Highway 128 is not a problem during the day. Highway 128 is a scenic wine route which passes many of the famous Sonoma vineyards. You are likely intended to spend an entire day on 128, tasting wine as you go, until you crash in your bed-and-breakfast. The road is far from stunning in the pitch black of night. It is the furthest thing from a shortcut that we could've taken. 12:30 AM arrived when we were about thirty miles from the coast. *No worries*, we thought. We'll just gas up once we hit the coast and make up time on Highway 1. We'll just sleep in our Holiday Inn with an ocean view a little later than expected, that's all.

There were countless errors of judgment in that last line of reasoning. Actually, you can't really call them errors in judgment, given that we had no knowledge of what we were attempting to judge. That was an error of judgment in itself, I guess. The rest of the errors were simply errors, large errors. The first error was my assumption of our ability to "gas up." That implies gas stations. There were no gas stations in northern California—at least not on Highway 128. And not on Highway 1, either. To say that we were prepared to sleep on the side of the road is an understatement. We had reached the point of looking for nice spots.

To cut past any suspense, we found gas. We found the station about a quarter of a mile before we were doomed. I don't know how. The neon lights just miraculously appeared and gas was no longer the issue. The new issue was making up time. How do you make up time on a road slower than Highway 128? Even though we appeared to be moving, it felt as if we were backtracking.

Take the point on the map which we thought we'd get to, turn back a page, keep following the road back down, and that's where we were. We gave up on time. At 3:00 AM all we wanted was sleep. Okay, this was the real error. How could we sleep on Highway 1 if there weren't any hotels? The answer: if you were a constant guest on *Life-*

styles of the Rich and Famous. There are no hotels, but there are plenty of places to stay. Bed-and-breakfasts, villas, chateaus, mansions—but no hotels. It turned out that Highway 1 is the damn Martha's Vineyard of the West Coast. People book lodging months in advance. They book it for three hundred dollars a night. My suggestion that there would be a Holiday Inn with an ocean view implies a Holiday Inn—and good luck finding one on Highway 1. We did somehow find a Denny's though. We stopped at Denny's to fuel our bodies and think. Our best idea was to sleep in the booth. The waitress was not about it. We asked. Seriously. Multiple times.

I awoke in the tent to the sound of the ocean in the distance. It was 7:23 AM. Upon discovering that my eyes were open for good, I took a stroll in the direction of the noise. What I found pleased me a great bit. When I pictured the northern coast of California, I pictured large, rocky beaches covered in fog. What I discovered on my morning walk were large, misty, rocky beaches covered with seals—an added benefit. Waves were crashing sharply onto the rocky coast. I roused the others to share. We spent the next half hour slowly waking up along the foreign shore. Time was not on our side, though. We needed to get out of the campground before the Rangers made their morning rounds. We didn't exactly sleep in a designated spot. We were definitely not about to *pay* for such accommodations.

The day ahead of us would be a long one. The heart of the Redwoods lay about thirty miles south of the Oregon border. Let's just say we were nowhere near thirty miles south. But it was Saturday. We were in California. None of us had seen the Redwoods. All we had to do was roll down the windows, pop in a few CDs, and we were there. What the hell else were we going to do? Sit at home and read a book? There are times for sitting at home and reading a book. This was not one of them. This was a time to drive. This was a time to get out on the open road. This was a time to set foot in a larger forest. This was a time to sleep on a new beach. This was a time for new sights and new conversation. This was a time for new. What a way to spend the last weekend. It was fitting, in my book.

A drive through the Nevada desert

Paul in the Desolation Wilderness National Forest, above
Lake Tahoe

Paul in Homewood, California (Lake Tahoe)

Will Beights on a morning sail

Ben Hoover on an evening sail

Skip White grilling out (as usual) in South Lake Tahoe

Hunter Jones in constant search of trout

Epilogue

Please don't be fooled by the word *epilogue*. My story is far from over. Life is just beginning. This is only the first chapter.

Well, I gave up. I surrendered to society. I got a job. As I mentioned, I now live and work in New York. So, I became a sucker like the rest of them. But you know what? I don't mind. I don't mind, because I did it my way first. I don't mind, because I'm still out there doing things I've never done before. When I look back upon my life, as the years go by, and as the winds blow, I won't be tortured by thoughts of a wasted youth. I won't have those moments of regret. No midlife crisis coming here. No, I will look back content, content that I tried. You see, I will know. I will know that I've been to the places of my mind. I will know that my thoughts and desires were possible. This is one of the few key lessons of youth. Because of this knowledge, my younger days will age with me. These experiences are now buried within my soul. Instead of facing growing discomfort and regret as I move onward, I will view peaceful memories and a clear forecast. I will keep my youth close beside me, and I will use it as a constant source of strength. In fact, I couldn't live without it.

Imagine that a pair of eyes on a man in his early thirties suddenly opened for the first time. These eyes, for whatever reason, did not see this man's days of youth. Even if these eyes saw all that the world would allow—for days, weeks, years, and decades, until the man reached a mature and healthy death, I would consider this man to have been blind all of his life. He may have known what it was like to live life as an adult, yet he would not have understood how he got there.

You see, this is not a book about travel. This is a book about self-discovery. This is a book about avoiding regret. How do you avoid regret? You listen to yourself. You listen to your thoughts. You listen to your ideas. And you see them through. This is a book about following your inner intuitions. This is a book about curiosity and the search for knowledge. In fact, this book is the same old story that you've read a thousand times over. This is the story of King Arthur and the Knights of the Round Table. This is the story of Jack and the Beanstalk. This is the story of Tom Sawyer; Huck Finn; Christopher Columbus; Peter Pan; Adam and Eve; Odysseus; Lewis and Clark; The Lion, the Witch, and the Wardrobe. The list goes on, of course. This is a story about trial and attempt. The attempts just happened to be mine, that's all. This is my attempt at travel, my attempt at writing, my attempt at, well, at attempt itself. This is not the perfect story. With trial comes error. But these errors add up to something greater. These errors add up to truth of self and conviction.

You know what I've learned about myself in the process? I now know what I want to do with my life. That's pretty important, don't you think? To me, it's simple. I want to travel the world, fall in love, travel the world with those I love, leave a positive lasting mark, help those who are less fortunate, follow my passions, and listen to some damn good music along the way.

What do *you* want to do? I have an easy question for you. Are you living your life in such a way that if you wrote about it, people would want to read it? Recently, I've found that to be a helpful question to ask. Would you want to read your own story? If not, think about the story you'd like to write. That will at least get you moving in the right direction.

You know at the end of the movie, when the camera leaves the face of the actor and zooms out so that you see the yard, and then the house, and then a panoramic view of the entire street? In only moments you end up staring down with a bird's-eye view on the whole town. It is at that point that you realize you've just watched one of the best movies you've ever seen. All it takes is one step back into a different perspective to see the greater meaning. There are often books released that one might expect to see on the shelves. I just hope this is a nice change of pace.

On the morning that I decided to write this book, I looked into the mirror and smiled. I realized that with an attempt, anything was possible.

If you tell yourself with a true and vulnerable heart what it is that you honestly want in your life, well, those things just might happen.

Even though I know what I want to do with my life, I still have no idea how I'm going to get there. But, as always, I have my ideas. That's what's important. All I know is that I'm blessed with a creative spirit. If I can keep putting my imagination to work, then I'll end up a happy person. I guess we'll have to wait and see what happens, won't we? Until then, I'm just sitting here in limbo, waiting for the dice to roll.

978-0-595-46249-0
0-595-46249-9

Printed in the United States
220900BV00001B/1/P